on track ...

Jack White
and
The White Stripes

every album, every song

Ben L. Connor

sonicbondpublishing.com

Sonicbond Publishing Limited
www.sonicbondpublishing.co.uk
Email: info@sonicbondpublishing.co.uk

First Published in the United Kingdom 2023
First Published in the United States 2023

British Library Cataloguing in Publication Data:
A Catalogue record for this book is available from the British Library

Copyright Ben L Connor 2023

ISBN 978-1-78952-303-4

Typeset in ITC Garamond Std & ITC Avant Garde Gothic
Printed and bound in England

Graphic design and typesetting: Full Moon Media

Follow us on social media:
Twitter: https://twitter.com/SonicbondP
Instagram: www.instagram.com/sonicbondpublishing_/
Facebook: www.facebook.com/SonicbondPublishing/

Linktree QR code:

on track ...

Jack White
and
The White Stripes

every album, every song

Ben L. Connor

sonicbondpublishing.com

on track ...

Jack White
and The White Stripes

Contents

Introduction

Who is the last great rock star?

This is a question worth asking, because rock – guitar-based music made by artists who write their own material and play their own instruments, in the tradition harking back to blues, country, and folk music – is no longer the youth-driven, zeitgeist-defining force it once was. Popular music's modern superstars (Beyonce, Drake, Taylor Swift) come from the worlds of R&B, hip-hop and pop-country – not from the world of rock.

This is why I propose that Jack White might be the last great rock star. He is a larger-than-life trend-setting iconoclast, who writes, sings and plays his own material. From his breakthrough band The White Stripes, through his work with The Raconteurs and The Dead Weather, to his current solo career, he has amassed a sprawling discography that runs the full range of rock 'n' roll styles and sounds. Along the way, he accumulated significant sales, critical acclaim and a dedicated fanbase. Now, as the head of his own record label, he is able to sustain his career outside the mercenary demands of the music industry. This is all the more remarkable, considering he began in a two-piece garage blues band. Of course, alongside those achievements, he has garnered a reputation as a musical Luddite, who paradoxically champions the 'purity' of older musical styles and technologies, while being obsessed with his persona and aesthetics. But that is just like a rock star: they should be larger-than-life figures.

In this book, I will be going through Jack White's discography album by album, track by track, in chronological order. All non-album songs – singles, B-sides, soundtrack contributions, etc. – I will cover in the 'Non-Album Tracks, B-Sides And Rarities' section after the main albums. I will also briefly cover Jack's appearances on other artist's songs and his production work. Jack is comparable to Elvis Costello and Todd Rundgren, in that while he rose to fame with an identifiable sound and persona, he challenged himself to try different genres and hybrid sounds, and his collaborations were an important aspect of his creative development.

This book is not a complete discography, so I will not be covering every edition of every Jack White album or single. That would take a whole other book! This is also not a biography, so I will not be covering Jack's personal history in detail. Jack is not a confessional singer-songwriter in the vein of Joni Mitchell or Stevie Nicks, where their music is a thinly veiled account of their private life. He is more in the vein of Neil Young or Patti Smith, using extended metaphors and fictional scenarios to convey broader universal truths. But there is a lot to say about Jack's personal philosophies and how they're reflected in his music, so we need to first explore where he came from and the musical forces that shaped him ...

Jack White was born John Anthony Gillis on 9 July 1975. Given his perchant for self-mythologising, it would be fun to say he was born in a remote log cabin while thunder rolled outside and a two-headed calf was born in the nearby cemetery. But no, he was born and raised in Southwest Detroit. But in a way, that itself was prophetic, for there are few cities in America with as storied a musical history as Detroit.

On the one hand, Detroit was home to artists such as The Stooges, The MC5, Grand Funk Railroad and the original Alice Cooper band, who made messy, atavistic rock 'n' roll that laid the foundations for punk and metal. On the other hand, Detroit was frequently at the cutting edge of popular music, from the world-conquering assembly-line production process of Berry Gordy's Motown Records to the cosmic funk-rock hybrid of George Clinton's Parliament-Funkadelic project and the trendsetting Detroit techno sound of the 1980s. And before all this, of course, was the original blues boogie man John Lee Hooker.

Detroit's musical eclecticism reflects its turbulent history. It was nicknamed 'Motor City' because it is where the major American car companies built their manufacturing plants. The city's rapid growth led to a population boom, with a particularly large Black community. But as the American auto industry collapsed, the city declined, and this intergenerational trauma left deep scars on the people. Among the more dramatic shifts, the more well-off white families fled to the suburbs, and so between the 1950s and the 1990s, the city changed from two-thirds white to 80% Black. It was into this arena that Jack White was born.

Jack's family was a large working-class Catholic brood. As the youngest of ten children – and likely unplanned – Jack had the feeling he was something of an afterthought. He had to accept every hand-me-down you can think of – clothes, toys, etc. This likely contributed to his ethos of taking what little you have and making the most of it. He briefly considered joining the priesthood or the military because it offered structure and regimen. He admired martyrs and saints for their dedication and sacrifice, and this fed into his work ethic. When he began to make music of his own, he started on the drums, a punishing instrument to learn.

At 16, Jack began an apprenticeship with local upholster Brian Muldoon. Muldoon furthered Jack's musical education by introducing him to underground garage blues artists. Jack and Muldoon began to jam together in a band called The Upholsters, but just as important was his upholstery training. Early on, Jack liked to strip his music down to the bare essentials, and then play as loudly and wildly as possible – like taking an old piece of furniture and making it seem new again.

Jack was an avid music historian, buying armfuls of vinyl records from local stores. This put him at odds with his peers at Cass Technical High School. As he told *Mojo*: 'The school was Mexican and Black and they were all into rap and house music, which I couldn't stand'. That led to some tension, but also a healthy respect for Black music. Eventually, he was led to classic blues artists like Skip James, Blind Willie Johnson and Charley Patton. He valorised artists who made music of great feeling and power with relatively simple playing and production. He found a copy of The Stooges' blistering 1970 album *Fun House* in the trash and fell in love with it. Other albums he admired were The Modern Lover's self-titled debut and The Gun Club's *Fire Of Love*. In terms of local bands, he especially loved The Gories. These garage rockers were a band out of time in their 80s/90s heyday, destined for obscurity, but serving as a bridge between Detroit's past and its future.

At this juncture, it might be helpful to define what 'garage rock' is. That is not easy to do, as unlike other rock subgenres, such as punk, prog, grunge, or hair metal, garage rock is not tied to a particular time, place or subculture. What defines garage rock is an ethos of simplicity and single-mindedness: rudimentary instrumentation and unpolished vocals, short, punchy songs, and no pretentious interest in 'high art'. The myth of garage rock is that it is closest to the 'pure' rock 'n' roll that only really exists in the minds of rock historians: music made for the love of making music, by working-class heroes whose passion and energy counted more than their talent or songwriting ability.

By the 1990s, there was a thriving, if insular, Detroit garage rock scene. The members of these bands all knew each other and played together, resulting in a febrile community of like-minded iconoclasts. These musicians were also crate diggers, bonding over rediscovered classics and forgotten obscurities. It was a point of pride for Detroit's garage rock scene that they made music for themselves and a small group of fans, the rest of the world be damned.

After graduating high school, Jack became the drummer for local band Goober & The Peas. They flitted between garage rockabilly and camp country cabaret, modelling for Jack how to transcend genre barriers in a constructive way. Their sparkly outfits also showed him the importance – and the fun – of thoughtful presentation. Jack joined the band 2-Star Tabernacle, sharing the singing, songwriting and guitar-playing duties with Dan Miller. After leaving them, he joined the hotly-tipped The Go for one album. None of these bands provided the right environment for Jack to express himself. For that, he would need a special ingredient...

Megan Martha White was born on 9 December 1974 and she grew up in Grosse Point, a more affluent middle-class suburb of Detroit. She and Jack were married on 21 September 1996. He took her surname, an unconventional gesture to be sure, but the resulting stage name was appropriate for his new band. Six months into their marriage, Meg asked to play Jack's drums, and the two performed David Bowie's 'Moonage Daydream' together. This gave Jack an idea for a band, so they set up their instruments in their attic and proceeded to write songs.

Jack had The White Stripes planned out conceptually before they even recorded a note. Jack said to *Mojo* in 2002:

> When we started the band, it was just some way of getting back to childhood without it being a comedy act. It was about how kids look at things. There's

a sense of humour that is deeply buried under everything. I kind of like it if people saw us and, just halfway through the steps, started laughing.

The imaginary backstory of the band is that a brother and sister discover musical instruments in an attic and start playing with guileless glee. 'Our objective was to be as simple as possible', Jack told the *Metro Press* in 1999. 'Meg's sound is like a little girl trying to play the drums and doing the best she can'.

Meg is regarded by some as the 'weak link' in The White Stripes for her untutored playing style. As recently as March 2023, journalist Lachlan Markay tweeted: 'The tragedy of The White Stripes is how great they would have been with a half decent drummer' and 'I'm sorry Meg White was terrible and no band is better for having shitty percussion'. This provoked a wave of righteous backlash from fans, as well as some enlightened defences of Meg's playing from The Roots' drummer Questlove and Against Me!'s Laura Jane Grace – an indication of the high regard in which other musicians hold her.

When people call Meg's drumming rough and rudimentary, their mistake is in thinking of that as a negative. Criticising her drumming for being simplistic is like criticising 'Sister Ray' by The Velvet Underground for being too long, or lambasting The Ramones for playing too fast. That's the whole point! There isn't a single song Meg recorded that would have been improved by Neil Peart-level skills or John Bonham-style showboating. How do we know that Meg White was the perfect drummer for The White Stripes? Because she was the drummer for The White Stripes.

The other 'myth' about Meg is that she was nothing but a vessel for Jack's music. While it is true that Jack often told her what to play and how to play it, Meg was happy to serve the songs – she did not want to be a superstar. Meg let Jack be Jack. She also had her own tastes – notably country music – and while she was quiet and not prone to overt displays of attitude, when she had an opinion, it was a strong one, especially when it came to deciding if a recording was up to snuff.

A guitar and drums set-up with no bass is unusual in rock 'n' roll. Jack once asked his friend Steve Nawara to play bass for a couple of shows, but the beat was so simple that all the bassist could do was follow it. Besides, the limitations of the two-person line-up appealed to Jack, as he thrives when he has to battle restrictions. As he said to *Mojo* in 2002:

I like the rules. When the rules are in place, it's beautiful to follow them or break them, but if there's complete ignorance of the rules, then it's just unhealthy energy. I like Nirvana, but after that, we just had to deal with all these watered-down rule-breakers.

In 2003, in the same magazine, he complained to Iggy Pop: 'What is it about modern rock 'n' roll, which doesn't capture the spirit of rock 'n' roll, it's just the thought of it?' Jack wanted to avoid that sense of detachment. As he said to *Uncut* in 2009: 'I think the guilt of garage rockdom brings a lot of people to irony. To pull off something like The White Stripes, a lot of bands would've tried to make it funny. We never did that'.

The White Stripes were named after the peppermint candy, which Jack had painted on the bass drum. The number three was also crucial to this mythology – one for Jack, one for Meg and one for the band, with three words in the band's name. They wore colour-coded clothes: red for anger and white for innocence. As Jack saw it, there's an element of respect for the occasion in dressing up on stage. He hated the 90s-era practice of dressing down for the stage, finding it lazy and disrespectful. The costumes were also a way to ward off criticism. As he told *Total Guitar*: 'All the aesthetics about the band and the way we presented them was a great way for me to get away with playing the blues'. By presenting the band as some kind of 'art project', he acknowledged that there was nothing 'authentic' about his music.

Jack's game-playing and self-mythologising might seem pretentious, but it needs to be understood in context. During the 1990s in America – the era of grunge, pop-punk, noise rock and lo-fi – hip musicians were expected to spurn any overt glamour and self-aggrandisement, to be humble, if not actively preaching an anti-fame lifestyle. They were expected to look and act as if they had just rolled out of bed and started playing music with their drug buddies in a dingy Seattle loft. The White Stripes stood out because they broke this mould.

That said, The White Stripes did not charge out of the gate with a major statement but instead released a handful of non-album singles on different labels (see the 'Non-Album Tracks, B-Sides And Rarities' section for details). These early singles were distributed by the small local label Italy, and Jack became their in-house producer. He recorded 7" singles for various artists in his home, using them as test subjects to learn the ropes of music recording.

Jack took promotion into his own hands by personally handing the singles to reviewers and mailing them to specialist music magazines. Eventually, the Los Angeles independent label Sympathy For The Record Industry, run by the eccentric Long Gone John, signed the band to record their first full-length album, and the rest is history ...

The White Stripes (1999)

Personnel:
Jack White: vocals, guitar
Meg White: drums, tambourine
With:
Johnny Walker: slide guitar
Producers: Jack White, Jim Diamond
Recorded at Ghetto Recorders and 'Third Man Studios' (aka Jack's living room),
Detroit, Michigan, January 1999
Release date: 15 June 1999
Chart places: did not chart
All tracks written by Jack White, except where noted.

The curse that afflicted most of the great alt-rock artists who rose to fame in
the 2000s is the iconic debut album that overshadows the rest of their work.
This is true of The Strokes, The Killers, Yeah Yeah Yeahs, Interpol, Franz
Ferdinand, Bloc Party, Ryan Adams and more. These artists have all had
lengthy careers and produced much great music, but their set lists, their radio
plays and their Spotify streams are still dominated by a handful of hits from
their debut album. The White Stripes don't have that problem, as this debut is
a solid but unspectacular effort, more interesting in retrospect for the promise
it shows than the quality of its songs. But it's a punchy, fun album with a
real sense of *joi de vivre,* a low-budget garage rock album with no pretence
of being anything else. Packing 17 songs into under 44 minutes, there's little
flab on this album. It was recorded at Jim Diamond's Ghetto Recorders,
a former chicken processing facility, over four days in January 1999. The
budget was $3000 and they only spent just over two-thirds of that. Jim
Diamond is credited as producer, although there was little to really 'produce'.
Jack already had the songs mapped out, so Diamond's main contribution was
capturing the band's sound accurately.

Why is the cover a banal photo in front of a garage door? It's because the
door had just been freshly painted bright red, and Jack demanded they get a
shot before the paint got dull. The bright colours would certainly have stood
out against the typical black-grey-brown designs of so many nu-metal and
post-grunge albums of this era.

In the lead-up to recording this album, Jack and Meg's marriage fell apart.
Jack even had his wedding ring digitally erased from the cover photo. It was
clear by the end of recording the debut album that they weren't going to make
it as a couple. As musical partners, though, their journey was just beginning...

'Jimmy The Exploder' (The White Stripes)
The White Stripes introduce themselves to the record-buying public with
a song about that perennial rock 'n' roll topic: a monkey that blows up
anything that isn't red. Who among us cannot relate to such a timeless theme?

Seriously, though, there is a tradition of songs about kooky animal characters, including The B-52's 'Rock Lobster' and Pink Floyd's 'Lucifer Sam'. If Paul McCartney can get away with 'Rocky Racoon', then why not 'Jimmy The Exploder'? There is not much depth to the lyrics unless you want to interpret the monkey as a metaphor for the revolutionary proletariat or something like that. But does it need to mean anything? This is a song for bouncing around the room like a child in a sugar rush.

This is the only White Stripes song credited to the band, and its unhinged gleefulness sets the tone for the entire album. Notably, the first sound you hear is not Jack's guitar, but Meg's drums. The floor tom and snare boom out, with the natural reverb making them sound huge. Then, Jack teases us with a lick that sounds like a wrapper being torn off, and away they go!

'Stop Breaking Down' (Robert Johnson)
Robert Johnson looms like a primordial titan over any musician who approaches the blues with a sense of reverence and responsibility. His mysterious life and timeless songs form the common clay upon which the story of rock 'n' roll was built. People searching for the 'real' and the 'authentic' in popular music can find reasons to discount any musician until they eventually work their way back and stop at Robert Johnson, the King of the Delta Blues Singers.

Johnson's song was originally released in 1938 as 'Stop Breaking Down Blues'. The Rolling Stones duly recorded a version of this for their 1972 classic *Exile On Main Street*. Wisely, The Stones did not attempt to imitate Johnson's sparse, haunted style. Any modern musician who tries inevitably sounds smug and phoney. Just as wisely, Jack does not attempt to imitate The Stones. Whereas their low-key version ambles along in a drug-fuelled haze, The White Stripes' version is an effervescent burst of joy. They slam in with a bouncy riff that returns after each verse to push the song along. Music-wise, this is a good example of Jack's ability to make the past feel new again.

'The Big Three Killed My Baby'
So far, we've met Jack, the garage rock party starter and Jack, the blues fan, but what about Jack, the songwriter? Well, he arrives bearing this song before him like a battle banner. This song was The White Stripes' first 'signature song', as well as the first song to reflect their Detroit roots. The 'Big Three' of the title refers to the three major Detroit car manufacturers – General Motors, Chrysler and Ford – and the 'killing' refers to how their corner-cutting, profit-hungry ways have resulted in sub-par automobiles that endanger lives. 'Everything involved is shady!' he cries. As he said to *Rolling Stone*: 'I felt I connected with what I wanted to talk about: my city and the evil it contains, the big three automotive companies'.

Beyond Detroit's industrial worries, though, this song presages some of the lyrical themes that would reoccur frequently in Jack's lyrics. The line, 'Better ideas are stuck in the mud', indicates his frustration with people who stick to outdated paradigms. The line, 'The motor's running on Tucker's blood', refers to Preston Tucker, an independent automobile manufacturer of the 1950s who was run out of business by the Big Three through shady practices and political corruption. So, this song is the first taste of Jack's fascination with outsiders who try to buck the system. It's no surprise that Tucker's story was made into a film by Francis Ford Coppola, another idiosyncratic artist determined to do things his way.

The music for this song reflects Jack's fixation on the number three: 'It's three chords and three verses, and we accent threes together all through that', he said to the *Metro-Times*. He also complimented Meg's drumming on this song: 'Her playing on 'The Big Three Killed My Baby' is the epitome of what I like about her drumming. It's just hits over and over. It's not even a drumbeat – it's just accents'. Jack's forceful vocals compensate for the lack of a truly memorable melody, particularly the way he spits out the chorus with real venom.

'Suzi Lee'

This is another childlike song, conveying something of the joy and the terror of young love. This song introduces two of Jack's lyrical peculiarities. The first is that it is not clear if he's singing in character or not. The lyrics frame the girl as the pursuer ('She sent me flowers with her tears burned inside') and the narrator as uncertain, even scared of love ('And you know what I'd do? I would run and hide'). This theme of women as romantic predators who intimidate their male targets is a recurring theme in Jack's work, but it's unclear whether this reflects his real-life views on women.

The other lyrical 'Jack-ism' here is his habit of 'framing' the song like a story he is telling the listener. The opening verse goes, 'There's a story I would like to tell. My problem is it's one you know too well'. That last line is Jack acknowledging that love songs are all-too-common, and he has to put his in 'inverted commas' to avoid ridicule. There's something charmingly self-conscious about it.

The musical hook is the slide guitar playing by Johnny Walker of the Ohio band The Soledad Brothers. Walker taught Jack to play slide guitar, and he took to it like a duck to water, following in the footsteps of blues legends, from Elmore James and Blind Willie Johnson to Bonnie Raitt and Ry Cooder.

'Sugar Never Tasted So Good'

This acoustic ballad is a highlight of the album. It's a measure of great musical artists that their acoustic songs are as intense and creative as their electric songs. See The Rolling Stones, Led Zeppelin, R.E.M. and Pearl Jam for examples. It shows that the band does not have to rely on power and distortion to bludgeon the listener into admiration.

This is another song about falling in love, and again, there's ambiguity. I interpret the opening title line to mean that the feeling of being in love has made sugar taste even better to him, like he's never had it so good before. But the following lines, 'Until her eyes crossed over, until her mind crossed over, until her soul fell next to me', sound vaguely sinister, as if he and the object of his affection were merging. Later, he talks about the woman's own thoughts being too much for her, but he also refers to her as a puppet master. Blurred identities, subtle put-downs and manipulation – these are all recurring themes in Jack's lyrics.

This recording was the B-side of the non-album single 'Lafayette Blues' (see 'Non-Album Tracks, B-Sides And Rarities'). It was not included on the original 1999 LP edition of the album but was included on the first CD and all subsequent reissues, which is why I'm including it here.

'Wasting My Time'
This song's twangy guitar harkens back to Link Wray, the progenitor of the power chord. But the lyrics are reminiscent of Elvis Costello, being based around a pun on the phrase, 'hanging on the line'. The first verse reads like Jack is hung up on writing a letter, while the second verse has him recalling something someone else has written. Perhaps it's a 'Dear John' letter, as the third verse ends with him laughing at himself as the other person leaves.

'Cannon' (Eddie James House Jr.)
The best riff on the album ushers in a series of random ominous images: mysterious chimes, fire, tanks, a cannon. It all becomes clear as they segue into a cover of Blind Willie Johnson's apocalyptic classic 'John The Revelator'. Jack discovered this classic via a Radiohead concert intro tape. The version he heard was an acapella cover by Son House, and it's House's lyrics that he sings on this. He also dedicated this album to Son House, staking his claim as a modern interpreter of these classic sounds.

'Astro'
Jack counts this song in, sounding like he has a mouth full of candy. Then the most rudimentary bone-headed riff kicks in and barely lets up for the whole song. This is the best kind of 'dumb' music: repetition, not for lack of ideas, but for the love of the riff. Jack came up with the lyrics for this in the studio, drawing upon the dance records of the 1950s and 1960s that exhorted the listeners to 'Do the dance': do the twist, the monkey, the frug. What kind of dance is the astro? No one knows, but it likely involves jumping up and down a lot.

Jack throws a curveball at the end, with references to Nikola Tesla and Thomas Edison. Tesla was a Serbian-American inventor who pioneered developments in radio, electricity and more. Many of his discoveries were dismissed or suppressed, and he was ripped off and slandered by Edison. A troubled genius, misunderstood and attacked by his peers, later vindicated by history. I wonder why his story appealed to Jack.

'Broken Bricks' (Jack White, Stephen Gillis)
This could be considered the first 'punk' song on the album. It's breathlessly fast and it sounds like the band are deliberately playing artlessly. Meg bashes her cymbals so much that it detracts from the song. The bell after each verse sounds like Jack ringing the alarm because the studio has caught fire from how hard they're playing. Compared to most US punk rock from the era, this sounds far more authentic. By the end of the nineties, bands like Green Day, The Offspring and Blink-182 had helped redefine punk as just another 'alternative' lifestyle brand, associated more with streetwear and frost-tipped hair than with genuine anti-establishment sentiments. This song instead harkens back to the wildness of The Stooges. Iggy Pop once said that The Stooges' sound was inspired by the machines of Detroit's car factories. That may have influenced these lyrics – co-written with Jack's brother Stephen – which describe a girl exploring the ruined industrial areas of her childhood.

'When I Hear My Name'
The lyrics consist of only ten words, but this may be the most psychologically revealing song on this album: 'When I hear my name I want to disappear'. Jack isn't even famous and he is already scared of the limelight. Ironically, this is one of the most musically extroverted songs on the album. Jack hollers like Little Richard after every line, while his blues guitar licks fill up all the empty space, saying a lot with a little.

'Do'
Jack, the thoughtful songwriter, returns with one of the loveliest songs on the album. How can such a simple and repetitive guitar figure generate such a bittersweet feeling? It's paired with lyrics that reveal the depth of Jack's social anxieties. He sings about not knowing what to say, having his words taken out of context or misinterpreted, and that he feels judged for not wanting to be social. The song ends with a plea for someone to just tell him what to do in social situations.

'Screwdriver'
This song is a case study of The White Stripes' songwriting process: Meg pointed at a screwdriver on the floor and said, 'Write a song about that', and Jack obliged. This was the first original song The White Stripes performed, and they did not alter it until it was recorded in order to retain its sense of spontaneity. This is the most dynamic track on the album, but it's also the most formless. Jack lays on the hysterical shouting and blues licks, but it all sounds a little second-hand. They demonstrate that they aren't afraid to let a song breathe, with increasingly long pauses between outbursts. They'd develop this approach to better effect in the coming years.

'One More Cup Of Coffee' (Bob Dylan)

Every rock band must eventually cover Bob Dylan, and The White Stripes were smart in getting it over with on their first album and picking one of the few songs from Dylan's iconic 1960s-70s run that hasn't been covered a dozen times. This was Meg's choice of song, and it comes from 1976's *Desire*, the follow-up to her favourite album *Blood On The Tracks*. *Desire* is an album of moody travelogues and meandering story songs (like 'Isis', which The White Stripes have covered live), and you can hear its influence on Jack's later songs, such as 'Carolina Drama'. Their stripped-back arrangement of this song accentuates its sense of loneliness, with some gothic organ being the only embellishment on their basic sound.

'Little People'

This ultra-simple guitar chug suggests that Jack is running out of ideas, as the album enters its final quarter. The theremin-like sound is actually Jack using an effect on his guitar. The final line reflects Jack's perception of childhood as a time free from social anxiety: 'There's a little boy with nothin' on his mind'.

'Slicker Drips'

Riffs, riffs everywhere, but no hook or melody to speak of. The lyrics express a general sense of paranoia and claustrophobia. Usually, it takes until the third or fourth album before a rock star starts ranting about the pressures of constant scrutiny, but Jack was ahead of the curve!

'St. James Infirmary' (traditional)

This folk standard, about a woman who was brought to an untimely end by bad behaviour, has been recorded by every blues legend, from Louis Armstrong and Bobby Bland to Eric Burdon and Van Morrison. But the most famous version is from the 1933 Betty Boop cartoon *Snow-White* by Fleischer Studios. In this cartoon, Koko The Clown is transformed into a ghost, who sings the song as Snow White is carried off in her glass coffin. Jazz legend Cab Calloway provided the singing, and the ghost's movements were animated by tracing over live footage of Calloway dancing and then twisting and transforming the drawings to match the lyrics. It's an arresting sequence, as Calloway's fearsome pain-wracked singing contrasts with the bizarre imagery. This cartoon captured Jack's attention as a child, and he references it with an opening cry of 'Oh Koko!' He also salutes Cab Calloway with a snippet of his signature tune 'Minnie The Moocher', familiar, of course, to fans of *The Blues Brothers* movie.

The White Stripes' arrangement of 'St. James Infirmary' is piano-based – the first such song on the album. It's a stomping one-note arrangement that works because the song has a portentous quality, as if death is one step behind the singer. Jack can't match Calloway's theatricality nor Bland's soulful tones; on the contrary, one could say his vocal performance is overly mannered. But his approach heightens the grimness of the lyrics. Like many classic blues songs, 'St. James Infirmary' is about facing up to the inevitability of death.

'I Fought Piranhas'

With its chilly imagery and 'lone man against the world' sensibility, this song is the closest Jack has come to an authentic Delta blues tune. Johnny Walker's slide guitar adds to the desolate feeling. Jack ends the album with the line, 'Yes you're all alone'. It's a strange sentiment to leave the listener with, and it seems incongruous in light of what happened to The White Stripes.

De Stijl (2000)

Personnel:
Jack White: vocals, guitar, piano, double bass
Meg White: drums, tambourine
With:
John Szymanski: harmonica
Paul Henry Ossy: violin
Producer: Jack White
Recorded at 'Third Man Studios' (aka Jack's living room), Detroit, Michigan, 1999-2000
Release date: 20 June 2000
Chart places: did not chart
All tracks written by Jack White, except where noted

The White Stripes wasted no time recording their second album, which is something of an achievement given that Jack and Meg split during the making of it. They officially divorced on 24 March 2000, but they decided to keep playing together. Jack produced this album himself, recording at their home on 8-track analogue tape. For most couples, this would be a recipe for disaster, or at least for a more fraught creative partnership resulting in less interesting music. But they were mature enough to see that they were better as friends than as lovers, and this album reflects that with the superior chemistry between the two musicians. Some see this as a break-up album, but I'm not convinced. If anything, this album feels less personal than the debut, with Jack writing in character more often. As such, you could say that he found his unique songwriting voice on this album.

While their debut did not sell much, it got them noticed by people who mattered. British DJ John Peel began spinning the band on the radio. 'It's the same thing I heard in Howlin' Wolf or Lightning Hopkins', he said. 'There's a looseness, but at the same time, it's intense'. Tony Ferguson from Auckland spotted the debut album on the racks – a testament to Jack caring about the visual appeal – and he arranged for them to tour New Zealand and Australia, securing their fanbase down under. They grew their audience the old-fashioned 'organic' way: through live shows and word-of-mouth. They stood out from the nu-metal and pop punk that dominated alternative radio, and the idea that Jack and Meg were siblings was a compelling 'hook'. It was part of Jack's self-written creation story for The White Stripes, but he and Meg acted as if that was true.

Jack's flair for presentation extended to this album's title and artwork. 'De Stijl' is Dutch for 'The Style', and it refers to an art movement from the early 20th Century based around extreme forms of abstraction, reducing art and design down to simple geometrical shapes, horizontal and vertical lines and primary colours. The cover of this album is based around de stijl principles, with Jack and Meg standing amidst red and white squares and black lines, dressed in plain white pants and shirts, which makes them look like citizens of a dystopian sci-fi world. The root of The Style was the idea that 'form follows function' – that a building or a piece of furniture should be designed around what its intended purpose is. This approach appealed to Jack's sense of discipline and order, and the idea that 'form follows function' is implicit in Jack's 'don't bore us, get to the chorus' approach to songwriting in these early days. If the purpose of a song is to rock out, then it should be delivered with maximum volume and intensity, and if it is to tug at your heartstrings, then excessive embellishments will only distract.

Because of this clarity of purpose, many White Stripes fans – especially those who discovered the band early – regard this as their best album. I disagree, but you could make the case that this is the 'purest' White Stripes album, the one where their sound, their aesthetic and their influences came together in perfect harmony.

'You're Pretty Good Looking'

This is Jack's first great pop song, featuring a hummable tune with universal appeal, delivered with passion and sincerity. It harkens back to the vintage rock 'n' roll era when three minutes was considered long for a single. With two verses, three choruses and a bridge in under two minutes, this works as both a curtain raiser and a statement of intent, for buried not-so-deep below the surface are a couple of lyrical twists.

'You're pretty good looking... for a girl' could be read in various ways. One interpretation is that Jack is engaging in some light 'negging' – couching an insult within a compliment. This is a defence mechanism brought on by romantic insecurity. He wants to be her boy, but 'that thought is sounding so absurd'. So he zeroes in on her defects: 'And your thoughts have been stolen by the boys, who took you out and bought you everything you own now'. In other words, she owes everything she is to the boys she dated before. The second line of the song, 'But your back is so broken', is likely a metaphor for her broken spirit.

There are other random references. The year 2525 is presumably a reference to the 1969 sci-fi-folk song 'In The Year 2525 (Exordium & Terminus)' by one-hit wonders Zager and Evans. Maybe that song's theme of a future where marriage is obsolete appealed to Jack. There's also the recurring phrase 'Linger on', which could be drawn from 'Pale Blue Eyes' from The Velvet Underground's self-titled 1969 album – an album which, in the early 21st Century, was revealed as the template of a hundred lo-fi twee-pop indie bands.

So there is a lot to unpack, and the album has only just begun ...

'Hello Operator'

And here is Jack's first great rock song, the single from the album. It opens with fanfare, then settles into a fist-pumping call-and-response between Jack's vocals and his pounding riffage. There's also a wonderful breakdown in between verses, where Meg ratchets up the tension with tapping drumsticks before The Hentchmen's John Szymanski enters on harmonica for an extra dose of trad blues flavour.

The song gets its title, and its first two lines, from the traditional schoolyard rhyme 'Miss Suzie Had A Steamboat'. This is the kind of rhyme where the final word of each verse is hinted to be a swear word that the children don't say. It's the kind of cheeky but harmless child's game that would appeal to Jack. The reference to the malfunctioning telephone could also be considered the first instance of Jack's technophobia. He references a few older, maybe more reliable, forms of long-distance communication – the mail, newspapers and birds. Why are people trying to contact him? 'How you gonna get the money?' he asks repeatedly. He seems to conclude that he'll have outrun his creditors when he's dead. It's quite baffling, but it's all the more fun for that.

'Little Bird'
This song is driven by classic blues lick, with hints of slide. The rave-up halfway through has the unfettered feel of classic Yardbirds or Animals records. Lyrically, the song is a trifle worrying, as Jack sings of wanting to catch a 'little bird' and lock it away forever. However, he sings this in a quasi-formal style reminiscent of The Kinks' Ray Davies, who frequently wrote from the point-of-view of unsympathetic characters. There is a long tradition in rock 'n' roll of men exploring themes of misogyny by taking on the role of the villain. It only becomes a reason to worry when that's the sole point-of-view that they write from ...

'Apple Blossom'
This song has one of the strongest melodies on the album. It starts out with a simplistic one-chord acoustic riff before the song unfolds into a sixties beat-pop pastiche, with a stomping 4/4 beat and piano flourishes. The song has an old-fashioned theme as well, with Jack acting like a knight errant ('I will come and rescue you') and offering to be the girl's confidant ('Put your troubles in a little pile and I will sort 'em out for you'). The song climaxes with the line, 'I think I'll marry you'. Jack's childlike sensibility means that he looks past the horny cliches of so much blues rock and goes straight to marriage. In 2001, The White Stripes were mailed a home video recording of school children from Kalamazoo, Michigan, singing this song, and Jack was moved to tears by the gesture.

'I'm Bound To Pack It Up'
Jack sings of a relationship that's over and says that he's ready to leave. The music is so perfectly bittersweet that it's hard not to read this as an autobiographical account of his and Meg's break-up. But of course, he didn't pack it up, and there's a lack of specificity to the words that makes

it universally appealing. Jack plays upright bass as well as guitar, with Meg on shakers, while Jack's cousin Paul Henry Ossy plays the violin. The violin has a thick, compressed sound – close to a Mellotron – that makes this like something that would have fitted on a late 1960s prog-folk album such as The Moody Blues' *In Search Of The Lost Chord* or Jethro Tull's *Stand Up*.

'Death Letter' (Eddie James House Jr.)
The debut album might have been dedicated to Son House, but this recording is Jack's ultimate tribute to that blues legend. He discovered this song on the same 1965 album, *Father Of Folk Blues*, where he first heard 'John The Revelator'. As with many blues standards, it was adapted from an earlier song, and, in turn, was expanded and amended by other blues musicians, including Blind Willie McTell. And no wonder it caught on, as this is among the bluest blues songs ever recorded. It is a lament for a woman the narrator loved but couldn't keep, and now not only is she dead, but he has to go view her corpse and attend the funeral with all the other mourners who failed her. The White Stripes' version loses the lyrics about reuniting on Judgement Day, but pointedly keeps the lines, 'It's so hard to love someone that don't love you' and 'Just hugging the pillows where she used to lay'. So, it is easy to read this performance as being about the death of a relationship more than a literal demise.

The White Stripes' rendition of this song is an example of sublimated passion. Instead of using the song as a starting point for instrumental fireworks, there's a rave-up section that conveys the sense of pent-up love and regret being poured out, and it never tips over into histrionics. That would come in live settings, where this song was a launch pad for Jack's extended soloing. The White Stripes performed this song at the 2004 Grammy Awards as part of a medley with 'Seven Nation Army', and it is notable that they used that opportunity to highlight their influences, rather than play a crowd-pleaser.

'Sister, Do You Know My Name?'
This is another charming song from a child's point of view. This song's title could be a reference to the game Jack and Meg were playing with the press, as the lyrics read as if addressed to a platonic friend or a crush rather than a family member. The crux of the song is the feeling of wanting a companion but not knowing how to reach out. The song ends happily as the 'sister' takes a seat beside Jack on the school bus. Musically, it has a simple stomping beat that occasionally feels a fraction too slow to really serve the track.

'Truth Doesn't Make A Noise'
Now, here's Jack in chivalric mode, standing up for a woman who's been treated badly. 'But the way you treat her fills me with rage and I wanna

tear apart the place', he cries. In some ways, this is just as childlike as the previous song, only now it's about a big brother stepping up to defend his little sister from bullies. The song is a thinly veiled tribute to Meg: 'Her stare is louder than your voice', he says about his famously close-mouthed compadre. He also mentions her 'Heart of stone' and her 'Tiny hands', as well as 'The quiver of her bones below'.

The overall impression Jack paints of Meg is someone that people assume is a delicate wallflower, but who has a core of inner strength. It's simultaneously noble and slightly patronising, an odd song for a man to write about the woman he's just divorced. Musically, this is the most dramatic White Stripes song so far. Jack comes across like a brooding Byronic hero, and the moment he bashes out some crunching power chords before the piano enters feels particularly gothic.

'A Boy's Best Friend'

This is the worst song on the album. It feels like it's wallowing in self-pity, as Jack sings about cutting himself off from the world. Even his guitar playing feels lethargic. The final line, 'A boy's best friend is his mother... or whatever has become his pet', seems ripe for Freudian analysis.

'Let's Build A Home'

For a change of pace, this is an uninhibited punk track. The best moment is Jack's frantic slide up the fretboard, followed by a frantic flurry of half-played notes. The lyrics are beyond simple, just variations on the title. But it is interesting that Jack's version of a come-on is not to promise sexual adventures but domestic bliss. The opening voice is a recording of Jack as a child reciting a misheard homily to his family.

'Jumble Jumble'

This song opens with another voice recording, this time from a Quebec radio show. The presenter sued the band in 2008 for invasion of privacy and it was settled out of court. The song is not really worth that fuss, as it is another shambolic song where the lyrics barely matter. It reads like a nursery rhyme written by a drunken hobo. The best musical moment is the call-and-response between high-pitched and low-pitched guitar notes.

'Why Can't You Be Nicer To Me?'

Somewhat ironically, the song on this album with the most self-pitying title and lyrics is the song that harkens back to the cocksure blues rock of strutting seventies bands like Free and Aerosmith. The three-note riff is ridiculously simple, but Jack and Meg's grasp of dynamics turns it into something special, and Paul Henry Ossy's violin adds some extra texture. This song dates back to the band's earliest performances, which may explain why it feels so unforced.

'Your Southern Can Is Mine' (William Samuel McTell)

This is another classic blues cover of a song by Blind Willie McTell, to whom this album was dedicated (alongside De Stijl artist Gerrit Rietveld). McTell stood out from other country blues artists with his use of 12-string guitar and his laid-back vocal delivery. He was memorialised by Bob Dylan in the song 'Blind Willie McTell'. When Dylan sang, 'Nobody can sing the blues like Blind Willie McTell', he was using McTell as an avatar of what Greil Marcus, in his book about Dylan and The Band, *Invisible Republic*, called the 'Old Weird America': the collective unconscious packed with arcane knowledge, eccentric characters and liminal experiences, which the folk tradition taps into. Jack said to *The Guardian*: 'Dylan could have sung anybody's name and he used McTell's to make a point that all these things have happened in the world and there is still somebody that's going to scream about it'. Jack's admiration for McTell runs deep: 'To be blind, Black and southern, he had a lot of strikes against him and his lyrics showed just how intelligent he was'.

This is an interesting song to use to make that point, though, as it is at the extreme end of the blues' misogynistic tendencies. McTell threatens a woman in lines like, 'You wanna get crooked, I'll even give you my fist' and 'Give you a punch through that barbed wire fence'. The jolly way in which McTell delivers these threats makes the song chilling in a laugh-out-loud way. It gets especially cartoonish when he says, 'You may be deathbed sickness, mama, graveyard bound, I'm gonna make you moan like a graveyard hound'.

Jack's cover heightens the surreal feel of this song. He does not change or update the lyrics, which is wise, because hearing a 24-year-old white boy sing these lyrics – especially after going through a divorce – is so absurd that it makes the whole thing feel like a lark. The contrast between the lyrics and Jack's own capabilities is supposed to be part of the joke. Jack is adopting a guise here, albeit the guise of a real person. Jack told James Oldham of the *NME* that he covered this song because 'All that machismo kinda interests me'. Jack recognised that the original bluesmen 'were huge drinkers and beat their women. Some of their lifestyle choices make me wish I was born in the twenties; at the same time, some of it was bad'. Putting aside the tone-deafness of these comments, it's clear that what attracted Jack to this song was how it contrasted with his own attitudes towards women and relationships. It certainly is out of keeping with his tendency towards courtly posturing, as expressed elsewhere on this album.

The album ends with a recording of McTell himself, taken from Alan and Ruby Lomax's Library of Congress interview with McTell from 1940, describing his pain from a car accident. A fittingly perplexing end to an album of fascinating contradictions.

White Blood Cells (2001)

Personnel:
Jack White: vocals, guitar, piano, organ
Meg White: drums, tambourine, backing vocals
Producer: Jack White
Recorded at Easley-McCain Recording, Memphis, Tennessee, February 2001
Release date: 3 July 2001
Chart places: US: 61, UK: 55, Aus: 36
All tracks written by Jack White

White Blood Cells was The White Stripes' breakthrough album, and for many, it is not just their greatest album, but it's one of the greatest albums of its generation. *Uncut Magazine* and *The A.V. Club*, for instance, named it the greatest album of the 2000s, and it appears on 'greatest albums of all time' lists from *Rolling Stone* and *The Guardian*. To understand how *White Blood Cells* came to be seen as a generation-defining classic, we need to examine it in context.

2001 was a pivotal year in popular music in America. By the end of the 1990s, manufactured pop from Britney Spears, The Backstreet Boys and their clones ruled the charts; hip-hop was fully mainstream thanks to the crass commercialism of Puff Daddy; and Jay-Z and techno artists like Fat Boy Slim and Daft Punk were tipped to be the next big thing. Worst of all, 'alternative rock' referred to the dregs of the post-grunge era.

There was amazing, forward-thinking rock music being made at the turn of the millennium, specifically in the underground emo, post-hardcore, alt-country and prog scenes. But this was generally being heard only by the rock cognoscenti. It was the mainstream rock scene that suffered from malaise. All the mystery, glamour and sense of adventure – not to mention sex appeal – had been drained from rock. And then along came... NOT The White Stripes – The Strokes.

Is This It by New York band The Strokes was the breakthrough release of 2001, and it caused a paradigm shift within the music press. Other New York guitar bands such as Interpol and The Yeah Yeah Yeahs also found an audience, and the combined impact of them sparked the sense of a general 'Rock Revival'. Around the world, there was a resurgence of stripped-down back-to-basics rock 'n' roll, from Kings Of Leon, Black Rebel Motorcycle Club and The Black Keys in America, to The Vines and Jet in Australia, The Hives in Sweden and The Libertines in London. Many of these acts pre-dated The Strokes, as did The White Stripes, but it was as part of this post-2001 wave that they cracked the mainstream, however briefly. Even the hit-less undercard included some pretty great bands with one or two catchy songs: The Walkmen, The Subways, The Datsuns, The (International) Noise Conspiracy, Death From Above 1979 and The Kills.

So, in 2001, the world was primed to embrace The White Stripes – and Detroit garage rock. But strangely, no other Detroit bands broke through to the mainstream. Jack blames the local musicians' 'tall poppy syndrome'. But perhaps it was simply that The White Stripes hogged all the attention.

And no wonder, as *White Blood Cells* was simply a cut above anything else. But it was not as if they radically changed up their sound or style. It was that they had the songs and the talent and struck while the iron was hot. They recorded the album in Memphis, surely the most storied music city in America. They did only four to six takes of every song, to preserve the sense of spontaneity. Engineer Stewart Sikes said: 'If Meg was happy with a song, we knew it was done'. Overall, they took only four days for recording and one day for mixing and mastering, which is part of why the album still sounds so fresh and unaffected, especially in contrast to the overproduced radio-rock of the era.

There were no cover songs this time. In fact, Jack explicitly 'banned the blues' from this album to avoid being pigeonholed. While it was impossible to completely extricate his music from its influences, the songs on this album had more jagged edges and discomforting undertones, with Jack's punk and art rock influences more to the fore. In fact, most of the songs on this album don't even have choruses – the riffs are the hooks.

One element still very much present on *White Blood Cells* was Jack's paranoia and defensiveness. The name of the album is intended to evoke the idea of 'parasites' coming to attack the band. The front cover features Jack and Meg pinned against the wall by sinister black silhouettes. On the back of the booklet, the silhouettes are shown filming the band while Jack and Meg are now smiling and posing in an overtly fake way, an acknowledgement that they'll have to play the celebrity media game, whether he wants to or not. Their promotional efforts often focused on the band's colour scheme and old-fashioned aesthetics, and this played into the idea of Jack White as an eccentric genius. Also, the idea that Jack and Meg were siblings persisted, and every time a new outlet 'exposed' the truth, it added to Jack's larger-than-life reputation as if he was a master of manipulating the press.

The band dedicated this album to Loretta Lynn, an act that would pay down the road...

'Dead Leaves And The Dirty Ground'
The album opens with ambient sounds of the band gearing up as if the listener was invited into the recording process. Jack roars in with a gloomy descending riff that feels like a storm coming down, and then Meg slams in like a thunderclap and the two lock into place with effortless swagger. There's no chorus in this song, but after each verse, Jack resolves the riff in a way that feels very satisfying.

Despite the downbeat nature of the song, the words are quite positive. Jack reminisces about returning home to his girl and the little things she does that he adores. At the end, he compares their love to the Holy Spirit, but his most potent proclamation is, 'Every breath that is in your lungs is a tiny little gift to me'. It is tempting to assume this is about Meg, but the song was written before they formed The White Stripes. Michel Gondry's video for this song plays up the relationship drama, with Jack wandering through a literal broken home, while Meg appears as a ghostly reminder of happier times.

While The White Stripes have bigger hits, this song remains the fan favourite. It was ranked their number one song by music critic Steven Hayden, as well as by the members of the online music database *Rate My Music*. I don't agree, but in many ways, it is their definitive song. No other song better encapsulates their unique sound and musical chemistry. It helps that this song has not been overplayed as much as their other hits, and so it still retains its aura of cool.

One fun thing to note: this song served as the template for the greatest White Stripes tribute ever made: the song 'CNR' by parodist 'Weird Al' Yankovic. This song is, in one way, an even more subversive take on the blues than Jack ever wrote. The letters 'CNR' refers to actor Charles Nelson Riley, whom Weird Al sings about as if he was an indomitable two-fisted man of myth, ala Paul Bunyan. By making a beloved camp icon the subject of a braggadocious blues song, Weird Al comments on the macho nature of blues rock, and how men like Jack keep that tradition alive by acting the part.

'Hotel Yorba'

This was the lead single from the album, and it likely did a lot to get new listeners into The White Stripes. It's still recognisably them, but in a whole other idiom. It's like a country hoe down without the violin. It's certainly the band's best 'drunken sing-along' tune. The lyrics once again reflect an innocent understanding of relationships – accentuated by the nursery rhyme-style 'One-two-three-four' chorus.

The real Hotel Yorba was a stone's throw from Jack's house and became a tourist destination for fans of the band. Apparently, The White Stripes are banned there for life, perhaps because fans left bad reviews, having expected too much from an old suburban Detroit hotel. The video was shot outside the hotel in a single day, and the scene in which Jack marries the red-headed woman was shot at Holy Redeemer, the church where Jack's father worked.

A live version was recorded as a UK single in May 2001 (see 'Non-Album Tracks, B-Sides And Rarities').

'I'm Finding It Harder To Be A Gentleman'

Here comes Jack, the would-be gentleman again. From his perspective, manners have died out because a girl wouldn't even be impressed if he held the door open for her. The audacity! Jack also offers to carry her across a mud puddle, but she complains, so he drops her. The song casts women as less capable ('Every single girl needs help climbing up a tree') and in perpetual need of reassurance ('Well I'm finding it hard to say that I need you twenty times a day').

On one hand, this song is a regressive throwback to old-fashioned gender stereotypes. A 2012 article in *The Atlantic* used this song as an example of his 'passive-aggressive romantic retaliations'. On the other hand, Jack is playing a character. As he said to *Rolling Stone* in 2014 in response to that article, 'There's a notion where you listen to Taylor Swift, and you say, "This is her writing from the heart about a boyfriend she had". But that's not every songwriter'.

On the other hand, in a 2001 *NME* interview, he did say, 'No slur on women, but sometimes they're attracted to really bad characteristics in men ... Why is that?' So perhaps there is a kernel of real resentment here. Ultimately, I think this song allows Jack to let his worst impulses out in order to exorcise them. Taken as a commentary on gender roles, the lyrics show how intertwined the ideas of chivalry and chauvinism are.

Musically, this song is another interesting change of style. A pounding piano doubles the riff and gives way to an electric piano at the bridge. So far, the album has a unified sound without the songs sounding samey.

'Fell In Love With A Girl'

This burst of manic energy was the band's first zeitgeist-penetrating hit. It seems inevitable in retrospect because it's such a fine song, but this could not have sounded more out-of-step with the era of bro-rock and plastic pop. It's raw, unprocessed garage rock perfection, packing a catchy riff, a hummable tune, and clever lyrics into less than two minutes. The song has a wordless refrain in place of a chorus, and only two verses with sections repeated. Jack is confused by how hard he's fallen for this girl ('Sometimes these feelings can be so misleading') and, while the pair eat some ice cream (the 'Mello-roll' that is referenced), he tries to reconcile his feelings with his 'logical' fear of commitment ('My left brain knows that all love is fleeting'). It's a well-observed vignette that captures a specific feeling perfectly; it's almost haiku-like in its precision. The girl in question is then-girlfriend Marcie Bolen of The Von Bondies – described as a 'Red head with a curl'.

This was the second single from the album, and it owes some of its success to its video, directed by French filmmaker Michel Gondry. He used models of the band made from Lego bricks and animated them using stop-motion (with CGI touch-ups). The video was a technical triumph, but it also perfectly captured the song's sugar rush energy. 'I wanted it to feel like a children's program', he said to MTV. Gondry would direct several videos for The White Stripes and use their songs in his movies. The video won three MTV Music Video Awards. Strangely, the band did not perform at the ceremony. Instead, the 'rock revival' was represented by The Hives and The Vines, despite neither being nominated for anything.

This song also has the distinction of being the first White Stripes song to have a successful cover version. In 2004, English singer Joss Stone's slowed-down pseudo-funk version reached number 18 in the UK charts. There was a whiff of gimmickry about it, but it's a sign of how well Jack's songwriting holds up.

'Expecting'

Jack sings of being under his woman's thumb. He is sent to Toledo to fulfil some unexplained demand, but on completing his mission, she is still unsatisfied. The implication of the final line – and the title – is that this irrational behaviour is due to pregnancy. It's unlikely that the song is directly about Meg, but you can hear her on the outro asking Jack to fetch something before his guitar cuts her off. While this is not a particularly deep song, it's a forceful piece of music, with big booming power chords. To my ears, the riff is similar to Hawkwind's 'Time We Left This World Today'.

'Little Room'

This perfectly realised vignette is secretly the key to understanding Jack's entire career. It consists of just Jack's voice, and Meg's bass drum and cymbal in a relentless one-note beat, which makes it sound like he's reading a manifesto. In only 50 seconds, he outlines his motivation and worries. 'It's about always trying to remember where you came from and how to get back there', he told *Mojo*. Jack is keeping checks on himself, but this message is applicable to too many artists. It would be easier to make a list of musicians who haven't compromised their sound and lost what made them special when they got too big or too famous too fast.

'The Union Forever'

This is one of Jack's oldest songs, written while he was still in high school – which makes it worrying that the refrain is the jaded, 'It can't be love, because there is no true love!' But, in fact, almost all the lyrics are taken from Jack's favourite film, *Citizen Kane*. He sings, 'Sure I'm C.F.K.', referring to Charles Foster Kane, the film's tragic protagonist. Of course, Jack would identify with Kane, and, by extension, director-actor Orson Welles, the ultimate bull-headed, hard-done-by Hollywood visionary. In one of the album's best moments, the song quietens down and Jack sings the birthday song sung to Kane in the film. After this, the opening refrain returns, now with added drama, thanks to the subtle use of organ.

'The Same Boy You've Always Known'

This song was written back during Jack's days as a producer for the Italy label, and he performed it with 2-Star Tabernacle. It is another love song, with supple guitar work and judicious use of organ, and in contrast to the preceding track, it feels deceptively optimistic. Jack feels like his girl takes him for granted because he hasn't grown, but he still carries a torch: 'The coldest blue ocean water cannot stop my heart and mind from burning'. But there's a hint of passive-aggression to lines like 'I hope you know a strong man who can lend you a hand lowering my casket' and 'If there's anything good about me, I'm the only one who knows'. Self-deprecation or manipulation? You be the judge.

'We're Going To Be Friends'

Many songwriters dream of writing a new 'standard', a song of such universal appeal that it transcends its author. A song like The Beatles' 'Yesterday', Billy Joel's 'New York State Of Mind' or Leonard Cohen's 'Hallelujah' that becomes a go-to for cabaret singers, talent show competitors, soundtrack programmers, street buskers and YouTube performers alike. With 'We're Going To Be Friends', Jack created such a song. There aren't that many famous songs about friendship, so he found a niche where a simple song was needed to capture a simple feeling. And there is no song in The White Stripes' repertoire that better captures a simple and universal feeling than this.

Over a guitar figure that even the clumsiest novice could replicate, Jack sings from the perspective of a child, who meets a girl – Suzi Lee, making her second appearance in a White Stripes song – and instantly thinks, 'I can tell that we are gonna be friends'. Together, they walk to school, collecting bugs along the way. They do show and tell, reading and writing exercises and then Jack goes home and reminiscences: 'When I wake tomorrow, I'll bet that you and I will walk together again'. It's an impressionistic vignette, sparse with concrete details but packed with reference points that people can connect with. It evokes childhood innocence – specifically the ease with which one could make friends just by spending a little time in a shared activity – with no adult cynicism or condescension creeping in. The only song I could compare it to is 'Thirteen' by Big Star – another short, simple acoustic song that encapsulates a particular feeling, in this case, adolescent romantic awkwardness.

Despite being so different from The White Stripes' usual crash-boom-bang sound, it became one of their most loved songs. Partly, that was due to its use in films like the 2004 high school comedy *Napoleon Dynamite* and TV shows such as *House*. Jack Johnson's lullaby version for the 2006 *Curious George* movie was used in a promo for the TV station PBS. It was made into a picture book in 2017, with the lyrics accompanied by gorgeous black-white-and-red illustrations by Eleanor Blake.

This was released as the fourth single from the album, and Michel Gondry shot a video for it using leftover film from the video shoot for 'Hotel Yorba'. It features Jack playing and singing while Meg sits beside him on the couch. They played it on *Saturday Night Live* on the first of Jack's five appearances on the show. It is the perfect song to play with or for friends. For example, having become tight with comedian Conan O'Brien, they played it on the last episode of his *Late Night* show. They also played it live with The Flaming Lips at a 2003 New Year's Eve concert. The Flaming Lips had previously recorded the song 'Thank You Jack White (For the Fiber-Optic Jesus That You Gave Me)', which was based on Jack's meeting with Wayne Coyne backstage after a Beck gig, in which he gave him the titular tchotchke!

'Offend In Every Way'

This gloomy song is one of the less memorable songs on the album, but it is a nice contrast to the preceding track, showcasing both the sunny and the glum side of the band on the opening of side two of the vinyl version. Lyrically, Jack complains again about the stress of 'faking it' for the sake of social niceties. He worries that people, such as the press but also his friends, will twist the facts to suit them. Was Jack complaining about 'cancel culture' 20 years early?

'I Think I Smell A Rat'

A vaguely Spanish guitar figure opens this ominous slice of paranoia. Jack seems to be calling out his imagined enemies, specifically the 'little kids' who are biting his heels. Is he referring to imitators? There weren't that many White Stripes wannabes until after this album. But this could be a general broadside against disrespectful children. He accuses them of 'using your mother and father for a welcome mat'. 'Get off my lawn!' says Charles Foster White.

'Aluminum'

This is Jack's first instrumental – or near enough. It features his wordless cry but is distorted to sound like a high-pitched organ playing underwater. It feels almost like another song slowed down. This gets my vote for the worst White Stripes song. However, it did lend its name to a project that recorded instrumental, ambient electronic covers of White Stripes songs, and that is quite lovely.

'I Can't Wait'

The guitar figure that opens this song sounds, for the first few seconds, a lot like Nirvana's 'Heart-Shaped Box'. If you're going to steal, steal from the best. This song has one of the most effective choruses on the album, with the 'Yeah Yeah Yeah' backing vocals in time with Meg bashing the drums. Lyrically, this reads like a vindictive post-divorce song: Jack can't wait for the girl to come crawling back so he can tell her off.

'Now Mary'

Initially, this sounds like another acoustic ditty, but then the power chords come crashing in. The combination of acoustic and electric elements, plus the skipping beat, give this song a bit of a swingin' sixties feel. The lyrics are also light-hearted, with Jack expressing frustration with his girlfriend's changeable nature. This is the only song on the album that feels shorter than it could have been.

'I Can Learn'

Musically, this song rehashes ideas utilised better elsewhere on this album, with a Pixies-by-way-of-Nirvana influence evident in the contrast between soft verses and a loud chorus. But lyrically, it is one of the most poetic on the album, capturing the feeling of not knowing how to proceed once initial romantic overtures have been reciprocated. The opening couplet is especially evocative: 'I wish we were stuck up a tree, then we'd know that it's nicer below'.

'This Protector'

Jack pulls one last surprise out of his pocket before drawing the curtains closed: a song with no guitar or drums, just his and Meg's voices. It could be about the pressure men feel to be the 'protector' of their family. But the mention of something 'coming through the door' makes it feel more universal. That line could refer to the pressures of fame, or to false friends, or the dread of coping with intrusive thoughts. It leaves the listener eager to restart the album and banish this feeling.

Elephant (2003)

Personnel:
Jack White: vocals, guitar, piano
Meg White: drums, vocals
With:
Mort Crim: vocal
Holly Golightly: vocal
Producer: Jack White
Recorded at Toe Rag and Maida Vale in London, November 2001 and April 2002
Release date: 1 April 2003
Chart places: US: 6, UK: 1, Aus: 4
All tracks written by Jack White, except where noted

By 2003, excitement about the New Rock Revival had reached fever pitch. It seemed as if every other week, a charismatic new band emerged with a radio-conquering anthem. Little did we know at the time that the wave had crested and it was mostly downhill from here. Many of the iconic bands' sophomore albums flopped, and some were condemned to one-hit wonder status. The White Stripes avoided this fate by doing the smart thing: they made one of the greatest rock albums of the decade.

Not that it came easy. Between *White Blood Cells* and the release of *Elephant*, The White Stripes did everything a hot young band should do to build their fanbase and win over sceptics. They maintained a website that allowed Jack to talk directly to fans and they toured relentlessly. They played four consecutive nights on *Late Night With Conan O'Brien*. They played at the Reading Festival, appeared on the cover of *NME*, had a documentary about them on BBC Radio Four and recorded sessions for John Peel's radio show.

They also changed record labels to handle their increased sales. One option was Sub Pop, the most storied indie label of the 1990s, thanks to the grunge boom they facilitated, but their contracts gave them first refusal on new White Stripes music. Jack avoided such typical clauses, which turned out to be a career-making decision in the long run. In the end, they signed to V2 Records in the USA and XL Records in the UK and elsewhere. Crucially, The White Stripes' music was licensed through Jack's new Third Man Records label, which he had total control over. This meant that the band retained the rights to their master recordings. They turned down big money upfront to make this deal happen. According to an interview Jack's friend Ben Blackwell gave to *Audioboom*, Jack said, 'We never took an advance. We paid for all the recordings out of my pocket'. This was because 'We only wanted to make money if we earned it'. Jack's motives may have been ideological, but it was a canny business decision that allowed him to eventually turn Third Man into an indie music colossus.

But first, they had to record a world-beating new album that lived up to all this hype. No pressure. So Jack returned to his first love, the blues. But not in the form of cover songs; this time, the blues influence was more fully integrated into the established White Stripes sound. But this would also be the band's most sonically diverse album yet: the hard rock songs rocked harder, while the folk-pop songs were more lush and romantic. Jack said to *Mojo*: 'We've only ever worked on songs one by one, treating each song like the A-side of a 45. I hate albums where everything sounds the same, just one gigantic blur'.

To help them avoid sounding like so much mass-produced pop, the liner notes read: 'No computers were used during the writing, recording, mixing or mastering of this record'. This is reminiscent of Queen declaring on their early albums that no synthesisers were used, to make sure that human beings, not machines, get credit for the work. As Jack said to *The Guardian*:

If we can't produce something that sounds good under those conditions, then it's not real to begin with. Getting involved with computers is getting involved with excess, especially when you start changing drumbeats to make them perfect or make the vocal melody completely in tune with some program – it's so far away from honesty. How can you be proud of it if it's not even you doing it?

Lest people think Jack was too hung-up on his self-imposed rules, this album has a broader sonic palette than past White Stripes albums. This was partly due to it being recorded outside of America, at Toe Rag studios in London. Jack dubbed this the band's 'English' album, and you can hear the influence of beat pop and British blues. Another theme was, according to Jack's liner notes, 'the death of the sweetheart', by which he meant old-fashioned notions of chivalry. As Jack said to *Mojo*:

That romantic idea just can't seem to exist these days. The entire world is wrapped around sexual ideas, it's become so free-thinking that a lot of the old ideas are lost ... Those roles are destroyed by mass communication, the internet, television.

Elephant indulged Jack's love of in-jokes and symbolism. The cricket bat on the cover is a nod to the album's English inspirations, and (according to Jack) the arrangement of items is supposed to resemble an elephant's head. All the 'e's in the title were replaced with '3's, and all '3's were coloured red. Most extravagant of all, the cover photo had six different variations, the most common being Meg's clothing: she is dressed in white on the UK LP and black on the US LP.

The band's hard work paid off when the album went to number six in the US and number one in the UK, and won the Grammy award for Best Alternative Album. It placed highly on a dozen 'Greatest Album Of The Decade' polls from the likes of *Rolling Stone*, *Billboard*, *The Guardian* and

Newsweek, and on multiple 'Greatest Album Of All Time' polls, including from *NME* and Channel 4. Over time, amongst millennial critics and fans, *Elephant*'s status has slipped relative to *White Blood Cells*, which is regarded as a more perfect snapshot of its era. But *Elephant* is more consistently loveable, with a lusher sound and a more upbeat vibe. I'll admit to being a little biased, as I discovered The White Stripes in the lead-up to *Elephant*, and it is a wonderful experience to buy a highly anticipated album the day it comes out and discover that it's even better than you hoped.

'Seven Nation Army'

You can count on one hand the number of 21st-century rock artists who have scored a crossover hit – that is to say, a song the average man on the street would recognise. 'Mr. Brightside' by The Killers could be one. Maybe 'Best Of You' by Foo Fighters. Possibly 'Sex On Fire' by Kings Of Leon and 'Lonely Boy' by The Black Keys. There are emo artists like Fall Out Boy, My Chemical Romance and Paramore, who had big hits within the shrinking bubble of alt-rock radio. And occasionally, the odd rock song like Ghost's 'Mary On A Cross' will go viral on TikTok for reasons only the algorithm understands. And then there's 'Seven Nation Army'.

The White Stripes' biggest hit was born during a soundcheck in Australia, where Jack hit upon the ominous seven-note riff. On first hearing this song, many people were confused by the lead instrument. Had Jack finally succumbed to rock 'n' roll conformity and abandoned his minimalist principles by adding a bass guitar? But in fact, the riff is played on a guitar, with Jack using a pitch-shifting effects pedal to get that low rumbling sound. Bruce Brand said that it reminded him of John Barry – listen to the title track from *On Her Majesty's Secret Service* and ponder the similarities. It has a sense of high drama one associates with a sweeping cinematic epic. The riff builds dread as if hearing an army around the hill. When Meg enters with her stomping beat, it's like a thousand feet marching in lock-step. Then, when Jack cuts loose on the guitar, it's as if the battle has begun.

The lyrics were written during the recording, and they're among Jack's most openly confrontational. The title comes from his childhood mispronunciation of Salvation Army, but he uses the term for the hoards of people now prying into his and Meg's relationships. As Jack told Jim Jarmusch in *Interview*: "Seven Nation Army' is about this character who is involved in the realm of gossip with his friends and family, and is so enraged by it that he wants to leave town'. He was less circumspect with *Mojo*: 'The song is about me, Meg and the people we're dating'.

Jack has had all he can take of these rumour-mongers. 'I'm gonna fight 'em off', he says. 'A seven-nation army couldn't hold me back'. Is there a better opening line for a song to get you pumped up to fight injustice? It's easy to forget when you're caught up in the rush, but this song has no chorus – just Jack piling on the riff. 'I wanted to see how powerful I could make the track without resorting to it having a chorus', he said to *Detroit Free Press* in 2016.

Bafflingly, neither V2 nor XL wanted to release it as a single, but Jack's contract gave him the final say. And he proved wise, for 'Seven Nation Army' reached number one on the US Alternative Airplay and the UK Indie charts, number seven on the mainstream UK singles chart, the Top 20 in Australia, Austria, Germany, Italy and Switzerland and on the charts in multiple other countries. The numbers don't tell the whole story, though. 'Seven Nation Army' has endured far beyond its initial radio play. For one, it was awarded the Grammy for Best Rock Song. It has been named one of the best songs of the century so far by *Rolling Stone*, *Pitchfork* and *Classic Rock*, and one of the best songs of all time by BBC Radio 6 and Triple J in Australia. Between 2010 and 2021, on *Rolling Stone's* critics and industry poll of the 500 Greatest Songs Of All Time, it jumped from number 286 to number 36, leaping over 'All Along The Watchtower' and 'Sittin' On The Dock Of The Bay' to land between 'When Doves Cry' and 'Tutti Frutti'! Closer to home, it was named the sixth greatest Detroit song of all time by *Detroit Free Press* – the second highest rock song on the list, behind 'Kick Of The Jams' by MC5.

So how did a song with such a menacing air and no chorus become so highly regarded? This is a rare case in modern music where 'the people have spoken'. The song became a staple of sporting arenas, where spectators chant along with the riff and stomp their feet – something to get the crowd riled up that isn't Queen's 'We Will Rock You'. The first to do this were the supporters of Belgian football's Club Brugge. Then Italy sang it during their World Cup Win in 2006. The practice was imported to the US, making 'Seven Nation Army' one of the rare 21st-century rock songs that is ubiquitous enough to lodge itself in the memories of Joe Public. Regarding this phenomenon, Jack said to *Mojo*: 'People say, "Oh, I bet you Jack hates chants of 'Seven Nation Army' in stadiums". But why would that make me mad? Are you kidding me? That makes it folk music'.

Mention must also be made of the video, directed by French duo Alex and Martin, who also directed clips for U2, Jane's Addiction and Franz Ferdinand, among others. The video is coloured black, white and red, with Jack and Meg set against a giant triangular backdrop. The camera zooms past them over and over, in time to the relentless beat. It's a masterclass in iconic branding, helping enshrine the image of The White Stripes in people's minds.

'Black Math'

Before the final note of 'Seven Nation Army' has faded, the swinging riff of 'Black Math' comes roaring in like an attack dog. This ferocious track amps up the energy level even further. Halfway through, the riff slows down to a steady chug. It resembles – and I'm only partially kidding here – the way metalcore bands include a brutal 'breakdown' section in their songs, to get the mosh pit surging.

The lyrics give voice to Jack's autodidact tendencies. He calls out teachers who emphasise rote learning: 'Is it the fingers, or the brain that you're teaching a lesson?' he sings. In true American exceptionalist fashion, Jack figures that he can do better on his own: 'Well, maybe I'll put my love on ice and teach myself'. Near the end, his voice takes on a distinctly Elvis-like cadence, giving the song a comical air.

'There's No Home For You Here'

This song blasts out of the gates with massed choral vocals. Jack supplied all the voices, over 15 takes, maxing out the capacities of the studio's 8-track recorder. Queen is an obvious reference point – think 'Bicycle Race' or 'It's A Hard Life' – but there isn't a trace of 'camp' in this song. Rather, it's po-faced and strident, both in terms of its sound and its message. Jack is sick of his romantic partner and tells her so with a vehemence that would make even The Rolling Stones circa 'Under My Thumb' think, 'Hmm, maybe this is a little insensitive?' But as The Rolling Stones proved, you can make great music out of nasty ideas.

The music quietens down for the verses and Jack's voice drops to a near whisper, giving a disconcerting sense of too much intimacy. 'It's impossible to get along with you', he says. 'Fortunately, I have come across an answer, which is go away and do not leave a trace'. On the bridge, he recites a list of things she does that have come to annoy him, including talking quickly, taking pictures and looking happy. It's here that we realise that this song says as much about the singer as it does about the subject. He's looking for excuses to get out of the relationship. There's an element of self-hatred to the song, a kind of 'I'll dump you before you dump me' mentality.

'I Just Don't Know What To Do With Myself' (Burt Bacharach, Hal David)

This cover of the Burt Bacharach/Hal David classic was first recorded for Steve Lamacq's Radio 1 Evening Session, and released as a B-side for 'Fell In Love With A Girl'. The White Stripes' version might seem histrionic compared to Dusty Springfield's, but all they do is amp up the innate drama of the song. They avoid the common 1990s pratfall of covering easy listening classics in a bratty postmodern mode. In the post-9/11 era, irony was out and sincerity was in. By covering a Brill building classic instead of another dusty old blues song, the band acknowledged that their influences included such straitlaced classicist pop. Burt Bacharach, the venerable easy listening hitmaker, had undergone a resurgence in hipster credibility during the late 1990s. He became an avatar of genteel 1960s mod cool – a 'safe' retro icon with no embarrassing politically incorrect baggage.

This was released as the second single from the album, and it reached number two on the UK Indie chart, which proved that the band weren't 'one hit wonders'. The accompanying video was directed by Sophia Coppola and featured British supermodel Kate Moss pole dancing in her underwear. It was too revealing for US censors and the video was banned in that country. Jack was unhappy because he had expected it to be more of a commentary on the sexual exploitation of women. 'We've insulted Burt Bacharach', he said in *Q*.

'In The Cold, Cold Night'

Meg's first solo vocal showcase is utterly charming. Over a dainty little guitar lick and some gentle strumming on the bridge, Meg sings in a blasé manner about the beau who lights her inner fire. The effect is reminiscent of The Velvet Underground songs sung by Moe Tucker, 'After Hours' and 'I'm Sticking With You' – disarming in its girlish insouciance. In the documentary *Under Great White Northern Lights*, she sings a slightly rocked-up version on stage in a lower register, and it sounds far less innocent.

We can assume Meg is also acting out a fantasy scenario because it is awkward to think of Jack writing lines like, 'I don't care what other people say, I'm going to love you, anyway', for Meg to sing back to him. Jack had another vintage pop legend, Peggy Lee, in mind when he wrote this, and 'Fever' is an obvious inspiration.

'I Want To Be The Boy To Warm Your Mother's Heart'

Jack, the gentleman caller, comes a-courtin' again with this genteel song. He once again harkens back to the days of courtly manners. At least he's talking to her mother instead of asking her father for her hand in marriage. Jack paints a subtlety hilarious scenario where the suitor's every effort to appeal to the mother has failed. Even home-baked goods don't work. Jack blames class snobbery, that he has neither a family fortune nor good looks. 'Somebody ripped out my page in your telephone book' is the kind of neurotic detail only a true romantic obsessive would notice. The real kicker is in the chorus: 'I'm inclined to go finish high school, just to make her notice that I'm around'. As with many of Jack's songs, this presents a child's-eye view of adult relationships.

'You've Got Her In Your Pocket'

This is one of their few songs not to feature Meg at all; it's just Jack and his acoustic guitar, which gives this ballad a timeless feel. If you told me this was a cover of a Nick Drake song, I'd believe you. It is another song about romantic obsession and fear of abandonment, but this time, it is written in the second person, with Jack admonishing another man for his possessive ways. The final chorus switches to the first person, and that could be the internal monologue of the man Jack is talking to, or it could be that he's talking to himself ...

'Ball And Biscuit'

Every great musical artist has one deep cut – an extra-long album track, a B-side or a rarity – that hardcore fans hold up against the better-known hits and say, 'This is their true masterpiece'. It's also usually a live showstopper. Songs like this include 'Blind Willie McTell', 'Jungleland', 'Ambulance Blues', 'Bad' and 'Yellow Ledbetter'. If there is a White Stripes song that fits that bill, it is 'Ball And Biscuit'. This song distils their sound down to its raw essence and showcases it for over seven minutes. Thus, it was voted the greatest Jack White song by fans on the *Rolling Stone* website in 2014, by a significant margin.

This song is based around a curt hiccup of a riff, perhaps the simplest riff Jack had yet devised. But in lockstep with Meg's steady drumming, it has a hypnotic feel: relentless and determined, the epitome of 'swagger' in two notes. And Jack shows off with some unabashed exultant soloing. As he told *Total Guitar*: 'It was a little present to myself. I let myself go'. As he said to *Sonic*: 'All was peaceful and calm when, suddenly, it was as if the Devil got into me and I could not hear anything except guitars. Fat, dirty, ear-destroying guitars'.

The lyrics are also dirty. 'Ball And Biscuit' is Jack's tribute to the Chicago electric blues style pioneered by Willie Dixon, Muddy Waters and Howlin' Wolf. Like such classics as 'Hoochie Coochie Man' and 'Mannish Boy', this is an exercise in braggadocio. Using the perennial lyrical structure of repeating the first two lines of each verse, Jack boasts to his girlfriend about how much of a badass he is. Smartly for a 27-year-old white boy, he keeps things largely metaphorical. The song's title comes from the nickname for the STC 4021 microphone, designed for the BBC in the 1930s. So when Jack says, 'Let's have a ball and a biscuit', it's as if he's inviting the girl into the song with him. Or perhaps not. Part of the appeal of classic blues tunes is that there is no one-to-one key to decode them. This song is similar to Robert Johnson's 'Terraplane Blues', which refers to a car, even though that is definitely not what the song is about. One true thing that Jack sings is this:

It's quite possible that I'm your third man child
But it's a fact that I'm the seventh son

He is indeed his mother's seventh son. According to folklore, seventh sons were born for greatness, which Jack certainly achieved on this song. If my word isn't good enough for you, consider that Jack received the ultimate accolade: Bob Dylan covering one of his songs! He and Dylan played a fantastically chaotic piano-based arrangement of this live on 17 March 2004 at the Detroit State Theatre.

'The Hardest Button To Button'

After the sturm und drang of 'Ball And Biscuit', you'd figure the band would quieten things down. But no, in comes another thumping down-tuned guitar pulse, introducing the album's second big rock anthem. It is an odd blend of gothic dread and headbanging. Jack takes on the persona of a child and sings with mounting hysteria about his family's new baby. There's something he's not saying, something wrong, but he never spells it out. The musical arrangement, likewise, feels as if it's continuously building to a blow-out that never arrives. To add to the oddness, Jack drops consonants on the chorus, snarling out 'The hardest bu-en to bu-en'. It's all very self-consciously eccentric.

This was the third single from the album, and while it did not have the same impact as 'Seven Nation Army', it was no slouch. It reached number eight on the US Alternative Airplay chart and number one on the UK Indie Singles chart. The single's cover art was a homage to designer Saul Bass, another pre-rock 'n' roll legend. Equally striking is the video by Michel Gondry. Using stop motion, Gondry makes it seem as if the band are jumping ahead with each beat along a continuously replicating line of drums and guitar amps. Beck also has a cameo as the man who shows Jack the 'box with something in it'. When The White Stripes appeared on *The Simpsons* in the episode 'Jazzy And The Pussycats', it was this video that they referenced.

'Little Acorns' (Jack White, Mort Crim)
This song begins with a trite moral fable regarding squirrels and nuts, read in a patrician fashion by newsman Mort Crim. This was apparently an accident: Jack recorded part of the song over a tape supplied by one of his brothers, which included this segment of a radio ad. The narration inspired Jack's lyrics, a message of resilience directed at a girl. Some of the advice makes sense, such as, 'Be like the squirrel' – i.e. store up your good fortune for hard times. Then there's advice like, 'Cut off your hair, straighten your curls', which is less helpful. This gets my vote for the worst song on the album: the squealing guitar tone rubs me the wrong way and Jack's 'oh oh ohs' feel especially affected (even for him).

'Hypnotize'
This song was written for The Hentchmen to record, but after two years, they had not used it, so Jack went for it himself. It is the shortest song on the album, with a brutalist one-note guitar solo, but it also has a solid melody. It is another telephone-themed song. How does one hypnotise someone via the telephone? Maybe Jack had just watched the 2002 horror film *The Ring*. There are also references to the classic hypnotist cliché of a swinging watch. The song climaxes with yet another old-fashioned declaration of romantic intent: 'I want to hold your little hand, if I could be so bold'.

'The Air Near My Fingers'
According to the good people of the internet, this song is written from the perspective of Norman Bates, the Oedipal antagonist of the movie *Psycho*. The evidence for this is the reference to a 'cheap motel' in the first verse, and in the second verse, he sings about his mother and how he 'can't seem

to think of another kind of love that a boy could ever get from anyone but her'. With this in mind, the repeated refrain, 'I get nervous when she comes around', makes sinister sense. It's a catchy song, if somewhat slight. Its main distinguishing features are the subtle keyboard backing and the fade-out ending – unusual for The White Stripes.

'Girl, You Have No Faith In Medicine'
One last furious basher. To my ears, the main riff is similar to 'Positive Bleeding' by 1990s cult act Urge Overkill. Funnily enough, their biggest hit was a cover of Neil Diamond's 'Girl, You'll Be A Woman Soon', which has a similarly formatted title – as well as a similarly patronising tone. The lyrics to this song were inspired by the placebo effect. In other words:

Is there a way to find the cure for this implanted in a pill?
It's just the name upon the bottle which determines if it will.

Jack is mad that women fall for 'alternative' medicines. Was he prophetically calling out medical denialism two decades before the anti-vax movement went mainstream? Sadly, no. He told *The Guardian* this song is 'about the irritation I was constantly getting with females arguing about headache medicine'. And furthermore, 'A guy can just put his coat on and run out the door, but a girl has to take 25 minutes waddling around looking for her purse or whatever'. Meg said the lyrics 'Makes me want to smack him'. Good for her.

'It's True That We Love One Another'
The album ends with Jack's Anglophilia to the fore on this acoustic three-hander. Jack and Meg are joined on vocals by British singer Holly Golightly. Jack wrote the song for her to contribute vocals, and since she lived two streets away from Toe-Rag studio, it was easy to arrange. The song is a self-conscious piece of role-playing, deliberately feeding into the tabloid speculation around the band. Jack and Holly serenade each other with puns and allusions. The wordplay is sometimes forced (such as rhyming 'able' with 'Bible') and sometimes it's charming, as in this verse:

(Jack) Holly give me some of your English lovin'
(Holly) If I did that Jack I'd have one in the oven

(Holly) Why don't you go off and love yourself?
(Jack) If I did that Holly, there won't be anything left for anybody else

Meg wins the song, though, when Holly turns to her for advice and she utters the line of the album: 'You know I don't care, 'cause Jack really bugs me'. The song concludes with Holly speaking off-mic in the most exaggerated British accent: 'Cuppa tea then? Jolly good'.

This song is a little too 'nudge nudge, wink wink' for some listeners, but it is a worthy climax to the album because, by this point, The White Stripes weren't just the most acclaimed rock band in the world; they were also the most *fun*.

Get Behind Me Satan (2005)

Personnel:
Jack White: vocals, guitar, piano, bass, mandolin, marimba, tambourine
Meg White: drums, percussion, bells, triangle, vocals
Producer: Jack White
Recorded at Third Man, Detroit, Michigan, February-March 2005
Release date: 7 June 2005
Chart places: US: 3, UK: 3, Aus: 3
All tracks written by Jack White

Søren Kierkegaard said that 'Life can only be understood backwards, but it must be lived forwards'. This quote applies to art as well: sometimes, it is only in the context of an artist's entire career that we can appreciate the risks they took along the way. Works that were dismissed in their time as self-indulgent or failed experiments can be understood in retrospect as the beginning of an artistic rebirth. And so it is with *Get Behind Me Satan*, The White Stripes' much maligned (at the time) and much beloved (as of now) fifth album.

Looking back on The White Stripes' career with the benefit of hindsight, it would seem like they peaked with *Elephant*. If this was a book solely about the career of The White Stripes, we would now be entering the big third-act crisis point. But this is a book about Jack White and this is where the real story begins. To put things in context, we need to examine two of Jack's immediate post-*Elephant* non-White Stripes releases. Coming in quick succession after his biggest commercial triumph, these helped ensure that he would not be solely defined – or limited – by The White Stripes.

The first is the film *Cold Mountain* and its accompanying soundtrack, both released in December 2003. Jack took his first acting role in this Civil War drama, playing a wandering minstrel. The filmmakers wanted a real musician for the role who could contribute to the soundtrack. He filmed his part in Romania in 2002, and he started dating co-star Renée Zellweger, which precipitated his break-up with Marcie Bolen. This relationship gave Jack his first taste of the Hollywood tabloid machine, which, of course, he did not enjoy at all.

The music was more important to Jack than the acting role. He recorded one original and four traditional tunes (see 'Non-Album Tracks, B-Sides And Rarities'). He researched the songs' history, opening himself up to the influence of the 'Old Weird America', as critic Greil Marcus called it. This indicated that Jack was capable of more than blues pastiche, forming ties with the 'alt-country' scene and setting expectations for his solo career.

Jack's other release between *Elephant* and *Satan* was even more significant. The manager of country legend Loretta Lynn noticed that *White Blood Cells* was dedicated to her, and played her their cover of her song 'Rated X'. Lynn invited Jack and Meg to her home, and Jack offered to produce her. The resulting album – 2004's *Van Lear Rose* – was a massive critical and commercial hit (see 'Productions'). The album proved that Jack could sublimate himself to another performer's vision, and it set him on the path to further collaborations and experiments; which leads us to *Get Behind Me Satan*.

While *Elephant* was diverse within the confines of roots rock, *Satan* went a step further into harsher sounds, greater sonic contrasts and more abstract song structures. While it's hardly Frank Zappa, this is definitely 'art rock' territory, where each song feels like a self-contained project. The approach was partly due to an accident. In August 2003, Jack and Zellweger were involved in a car crash, and Jack broke his middle finger in five places. He allowed footage of his surgery to be played on the band's website, with White Stripes music playing in the background. Afterwards, he could not play guitar for a while, which may explain this album's higher ratio of piano and percussion-based songs.

This is also the first White Stripes album that sounds as if it was recorded in a digital world, where music can be tweaked and processed to get the sound just right. Because the songs sound so deliberately constructed, there is a sense that Meg was less essential to the writing process. This is especially true of the softer songs, which sound more than ever like 'Jack White featuring Meg'. Nonetheless, she makes her presence felt on the harder and more upbeat numbers.

The prevailing mood is downbeat, though. Jack was in a dark frame of mind when he wrote this album. He broke up with Zellweger in September 2004 and chafed at the increased scrutiny from a more critical press and nosey fans. Hollywood legend Rita Hayworth was a reference point. Jack was fascinated by how she adopted her stage name to hide her Latina heritage. Jack saw in that act a microcosm of how the pressures of celebrity culture can warp a person's sense of self.

As if to confirm his fears, when Jack and Meg returned to Detroit to record this album, he found that his former allies in the garage rock scene resented his success. Jim Diamond even sued him, claiming he produced The White Stripes' first two albums. 'He's ruined one of the more beautiful things that happened in his life, the family of Detroit musicians he was a part of', said Jack to *Mojo*. He continued:

My mistake is, I continued living where I'm from – Detroit – after I got successful. You're not supposed to do that. I lost a lot of friends, a lot of people burned us … It seems like the family of musicians that we found, that I'd loved and that had increased us, had, in some cases, turned it back on me… I wanted to know why they hated me so much.

This led Jack to write from the perspective of various unsavoury and unsympathetic characters – putting himself in the mind of his enemies. He also titled the album after his favourite saying of Jesus. In Luke 4:8, Jesus says this when rejecting the devil's temptation of power. Jack said to *Mojo*:

> It's super appropriate for everything the album is talking about. It can mean you're either for me or against me. And if you're not going to help me, get out of my way. Or maybe it relates to the Devil's music, and having the Devil back you up while you're playing it. Or, perhaps, it relates to aiming for the truth, for doing the right thing and telling the Devil to take his temptations away.

The album artwork was their most stylish yet. Jack and Meg stand back-to-back in dashing costumes, with stricken faces, as if they've been forbidden from talking. Their fingers are outstretched behind them as if they are aching for human contact. As striking as the image is, it sets an arch, affected tone for the album. Noel Gallagher memorably said that Jack looked like 'Zorro on doughnuts'.

This was the first White Stripes album to get a mixed reception. *Mojo*'s review was especially harsh, saying, 'Jack White has built his first folly'. The consensus was that the band didn't play to their strengths. Most assumed that this album was a momentary misstep, and Jack would soon right the boat with a more conventional return to form. Meanwhile, those of us who appreciated Jack's more uninhibited and unfiltered side took this album to heart. For every artist, there is that one album which is like a 'cult within a cult' that hardcore fans defend to the death, even while acknowledging its flaws. For White Stripes fans, this is that album.

'Blue Orchid'

Jack credits the 'Blue Orchid' riff with turning the album around. 'The riff was so simple, so effective, it cemented the album together', he said to *Mojo*. 'It really rescued our mentality at the time, too, because we were about ready to jack it all in'. It also sets the tone for the entire album: expect the unexpected. After a short percussive prelude that sounds like footsteps racing down the hall, Jack kicks in the door with an in-your-face riff. But his guitar sounds compressed, with all the natural 'feel' squeezed out. His playing is machine-like in its precision, closer to the industrial rock of Nine Inch Nails than to the blues.

And the surprises don't stop with the music. Jack sings the bulk of the song in a strained falsetto as if he's trying to get the words out before he faints. The lyrics are dark and paranoid, establishing a theme that carries through the entire album. The opening line – 'You got a reaction, didn't you?' – smacks of passive-aggressiveness. Here, it's directed at a lover who ruined a good thing – 'You took a white orchid, turned it blue'. But it could just as easily be directed at those pesky journalists and hangers-on who keep bugging him.

This was released as the first single from the album, with different editions of the single featuring different people dressed up as Jack and Meg on the album's cover. The promo video featured the statuesque red-headed model Karen Elson wandering like a ghost through a rundown manor. Three weeks after the shoot for the video, on 1 June 2005, she and Jack were married. The ceremony was held in the Amazon jungle, officiated by a shaman, while Meg was maid of honour. They followed this with a Catholic blessing, and then a proper ceremony in Nashville.

'The Nurse'
Listeners perturbed by the artificial-sounding 'Blue Orchid' will find no solace in this, for it is off-putting in an entirely different way. The lead instrument is marimba, played by Jack. A sound more often associated with upbeat Latin American music is here used to sinister effect. The precise notes evoke the feeling of someone creeping around, up to no good. But then they're interrupted by violent bursts of noise. This song is guaranteed to startle a first-time listener – especially if they're wearing headphones.

The lyrics were inspired by Rita Hayworth's Alzheimer's-ridden last days, but they have a biographical element. Jack said to *Mojo*: "The Nurse' is about somebody I was in love with, had to be in love with for over a decade, but the way you explore all these characters compels you to know yourself better'. So, he explored a scenario straight out of a gothic melodrama, where a person is abused by the one caring for them. 'The nurse should not be the one who puts salt in your wounds', he whispers. That's a clever metaphor for an abusive co-dependent relationship.

'My Doorbell'
This gets my vote for Jack's best straight-ahead, no-frills pop song. The piano and drums arrangement is simplicity itself, and it demonstrates the pair's ability to lock into a groove. The refrain 'I've been thinkin' about my doorbell, when you gonna ring it?' has the purity of those classic Motown songs, wherein a single evocative idea is developed to its fullest. Jack is tired of waiting for his girl to come calling, and by the end, he sounds like he's trying to convince himself he doesn't need her: 'I've got plenty of my own friends, they're all above me'.

This was the second single from the album. It should have been a bigger hit, and maybe would have been if it had been released first instead of 'Blue Orchid'. The black-and-white video features the band performing for a small army of mid-century street urchins.

'Forever For Her (Is Over For Me)'
This is another piano-based song – a ballad this time. The blunt melody tightly follows the rudimentary chord sequence, but Jack's marimba and

Meg's cymbals give it some sense of delicacy. Even as the playing and singing become more intense near the end, the song retains its genteel feel, despite Jack singing about a relationship he knows is doomed.

'Little Ghost'

You can hear the influence of Jack's *Cold Mountain* work on this mandolin-driven hoe-down about falling in love with a ghost. It could be a metaphor for a one-sided parasocial relationship, but the song works when taken at face value, as the theme fits the Southern Gothic feel of the album. The term 'Southern Gothic' encompasses a wide range of literature, music and art focused on life in the post-Reconstruction American South. From the literary fiction of William Faulkner and Tennessee Williams, to the pulp potboilers of V.C. Andrews and Anne Rice, the Southern Gothic genre ruminates on insular and eccentric communities filled with desperate people trapped by circumstances not of their own making, and driven by obsessive fixations towards dark endings.

Whether or not Jack was directly inspired by these works, the American Gothic sensibility pervades modern blues and country music so thoroughly that it can't be avoided.

Jack's vocals are layered in a disharmonious manner that makes it seem as if he's leading a drunken barn dance singalong. The acapella break sounds especially sloppy, but that just adds to the homegrown feel.

'The Denial Twist'

Dancing as a metaphor for sex? What will Jack think of next?! This song starts dramatically, with Jack giving advice to a would-be ladies' man:

If you think that a kiss is all in the lips
C'mon, you got it all wrong, man
And if you think that our dance was all in the hips
Oh well, then do the twist

But this song feels nothing like 'The Twist', the 1960 Chubby Checker novelty classic. It sounds more like a dirty saloon getting rowdy after dark. Jack pounds his piano and hollers, while Meg navigates the tempo and volume changes with ease. There is also a more pronounced bass line – actually another down-tuned guitar.

The 'dance' Jack refers to is around the truth. He believes that it needs to be spoken for a relationship to mend. Whether or not Jack is speaking from experience, he crafted one of his best sets of lyrics. Two of my favourite passages are:

If you think holding hands is all in the fingers,
Grab hold of the soul where the memory lingers

47

and:

> So now you're mad, denying the truth
> And it's hidden in the wisdom in the back of your tooth
> Ya need ta spit it out, in a telephone booth

This was the third single from the album, and it had another excellent video directed by Michel Gondry. It features the band performing on the Conan O'Brien show, but they and the sets change proportions as the camera follows them, seeming to stretch and squash in real time. During their UK tour for this album, concertgoers could purchase a freshly burned CDR copy of each night's performance of this song immediately after the show.

'White Moon'

This song is musically slight but lyrically interesting. The music is based around a repetitive piano figure and nuanced percussion. The most startling moment is Meg's set of bells accidentally tipping over at 3:44. The lyrics have Jack reminiscing over friends and lovers gone, which made it the perfect song to end the band's elegiac documentary *Under Great White Northern Lights* (see 'Videos').

The line, 'It's the truth and it don't make a noise', references the similarly titled song from *De Stijl*. This song was originally titled 'White Moon And The Red Headed Guest', and that last phrase could refer to Marcie Bolen or to Rita Hayworth (who is mentioned in the lyrics). Or she could be a symbol of the ultimate unattainable woman – as for Charlie Brown in *Peanuts*.

'Instinct Blues'

Believe it or not, this is only the second White Stripes song with 'Blues' in the title – after the non-album single 'Lafayette Blues' (see 'Non-Album Tracks, B-Sides And Rarities'). It is a throwback blues jam with an old-fashioned lyrical list structure. Following Cole Porter's 'Let's Fall In Love' and its immortal refrain 'Birds do it, bees do it', Jack lists various animals that 'Get it'. By that, he means they make love, humankind's oldest instinct. Fittingly, the music is brutal, atavistic even – the kind of blues a caveman might have played, all pounding downbeats and raw power chords. It was used to good effect during an incredible stop-motion animation dream sequence in Michel Gondry's whimsical film *The Science Of Sleep*.

'Passive Manipulation'

Meg's brief showcase – just her voice and subtle percussion – is a plea to women everywhere to listen to their mothers rather than the men in their lives. 'You need to know the difference, between a father and a lover', she says. One wonders if Jack is projecting his own Freudian fears onto the women in his life...

'Take, Take, Take'

This piano ballad is the bitterest song Jack has written so far. He projects himself into the mind of an obsessive fan – of Rita Hayworth, naturally – who encounters her and turns creepy. The fan gradually gets more entitled, asking first for an autograph, then a picture, then a lock of hair: 'That was all that I needed'. The fan keeps insisting that he would be content if he only had a little more of his idol. Jack's contention is that if you give an inch of yourself, these parasites will only ask for more. Hence the chorus, which is simply the phrase 'Take! Take! Take!' repeated with increasing hysteria. He insisted to *Mojo*:

> I can think of something more interesting to write about than how terrible it is to be famous. It's more about how kids today aren't taught how to be humble or when enough is enough. I'm not whining about being a celebrity; I'm whining about parents not teaching their kids manners.

'Ugly As I Seem'

This song's off-the-cuff feel – with Jack on acoustic guitar and Meg on box percussion – disguises some dark lyrical themes. Jack reminisces about childhood again, but this time, it does not seem idyllic. He recalls children laughing at his Halloween costume and blood on the ground, perhaps after a fight. The chorus is among Jack's most ominous pronouncements:

> I am as ugly as I seem
> Worse than all your dreams
> Could ever make me

The music is far from ugly, though. The jaunty guitar arpeggios after each verse are especially appealing. The disconnect between the lovely tune and the self-deprecating lyrics makes this song fascinating.

'Red Rain'

This song has no relation to the Peter Gabriel song of the same name, except that they share an inspiration: the Book of Revelation, which includes blood rain as a harbinger of the apocalypse. Jack's vocals start out tentatively as if he's peeking out from under his blankets to check if the monsters are still there. His guitar pokes and prods at the darkness until he finally explodes with biblical fury, like an exorcist confronting a demon. It's not much of a song, but it is a great performance.

'I'm Lonely (But I Ain't That Lonely Yet)'

The album closes with another song about a failed relationship but in a more conventionally appealing and earnest style. With its stately piano and fluid melody, this could have been recorded in the early 1970s by Carole King or James Taylor.

The most striking line is, 'And I love my sister, Lord knows how I've missed her'. I interpret this line as Jack longing to be back in his 'little room' once more when it was just him and Meg playing small shows for local fans. But then there's the line, 'Sometimes I get jealous of all her little pets'. Could it be that Jack is jealous that Meg has fans of her own?

There is also more Biblical imagery, with Jack evoking Southern Baptist rituals:

I went down to the river filled with regret
I looked down and I wondered if there was any reason left
I left just before my lungs could get wet

You could interpret those lines as expressing suicidal thoughts, but I see it as Jack feeling desperate for meaning in his life. It's an appropriate way to end an album that sees him grappling with his newfound fame whilst tentatively exploring new musical avenues.

Broken Boy Soldiers (2006)

Personnel:
Brendan Benson: vocals, guitar, keyboards
Patrick Keeler: drums
Jack Lawrence: bass guitar, backing vocals
Jack White: vocals, guitar, keyboards
Producer: Brendan Benson & Jack White
Recorded at Le Grande, Detroit, Michigan, 2005
Release date: 16 May 2006
Chart places: US: 7, UK: 2, Aus: 14
All tracks written by Brendan Benson and Jack White

If the successive releases of *Cold Mountain*, *Van Lear Rose* and *Get Behind Me Satan* had not yet convinced people that Jack was on a major creative hot streak, then the revelation that he had a whole other band surely must have. In fact, *Get Behind Me Satan* was recorded in between sessions for Jack's new Detroit 'supergroup', The Raconteurs. For the recording of *Van Lear Rose*, Jack employed bassist Jack Lawrence and drummer Patrick Keeler from The Greenhornes. They worked together so well that Jack revived an idea: collaborating with singer-songwriter Brendan Benson.

Benson is a Michigan native whose stock-in-trade was rough but friendly power pop. If you'd like a taste of his solo work, I recommend his 2005 album *The Alternative To Love*. He spent the 1990s trying to make it in Los Angeles, and when that failed, he returned to Detroit and hid himself away for five years. His musical style was dissimilar to the local garage rock scene, but Jack was a fan – they did a 'song swap' one night in 1999, performing each other's songs on stage. They also performed in a band with The Waxwings' Kevin Peyok on bass and The Dirtbomb's Ben Blackwell on drums, workshopping songs that Jack would later record with The White Stripes. He also opened for The White Stripes on their early 2002 tour of the US east coast. Then, when the opportunity to form a band with Jack came, it was not just a new creative outlet, it was a way out of the funk he had sunk into. 'The Raconteurs re-socialised me', he told Jack's biographer Nick Hasted.

It was a new opportunity for Jack as well. As he said to *The Times*' Mark Edwards: 'This band will show that there are a few misconceptions about me'. This would be the first time since The Go's debut album that he recorded as a member of a democratic group. As Jack said to *Mojo* in 2006:

I keep my rules to myself in this band! No, I do feel liberated. I've always thought that beauty is either in defining the rules or breaking the rules. It's only scary in the absence of any rules at all. For me personally, there's a lot of breaking the rules here, of my mindset of the last ten years.

The album's brief was to 'avoid the expected' and not rehash each member's personal sound in a band setting. They wanted a sound that was more than the sum of its parts. Jack continued:

> It's funny; people who heard the record instinctively think certain things come from certain people. And it's always wrong. Like, 'Oh, that's obviously one of your riffs Jack'. No, it's Brendan's riff. Or, 'Brendan is awesome on the synthesiser on that track'. No, I play all the synthesisers on the record, which I've never done before.

The band built a strong live reputation, playing 70 gigs in 2006, including supporting Bob Dylan on eight dates. Importantly, they established themselves as a proper band in their own right and not just a Jack White side project.

The cover depicted the band trying to look casual after having been beaten up. Perhaps they anticipated a negative reception? But they needn't have worried. *Broken Boy Soldiers* was well-received, critically and commercially. *Mojo* even named it the greatest album of the year. I might not go that far, but it is one of my personal favourites. It combines elements of blues, folk, country and art rock into sunny power pop, with just enough underlying darkness to make it interesting.

Incidentally, Australians might be asking, 'Who are The Raconteurs? Surely you mean The Saboteurs?' Yes, indeed, the band are known by a different name down under, as there was already a local band called The Raconteurs. It is still difficult to search for this band on streaming services in my home country!

'Steady, As She Goes'

The Raconteurs introduce themselves not with a big flourish, but with patient showmanship. First, the drums enter, then the bass, then the simplest of guitar riffs. It sounds methodical, but the players' exuberance is palpable. Compared to the tortured genesis of many 'supergroup' collaborations, this song came together effortlessly. Jack visited Benson's attic studio and Benson played him the opening lyrics: 'Find yourself a girl, and settle down'. Jack added the title phrase, and they were off to the races. Benson said to *Mojo* in 2006:

> We stood back and thought, fucking hell, this is great! I felt it was the motivation for the whole thing, that one song. To hear us singing together, for me to hear myself singing along with Jack, was a big thrill. And to hear it sound nice was more fuel to the fire – let's do this.

They brought in Lawrence and Keeler and recorded the song on the second take. And thus, The Raconteurs were born!

Jack and Benson sing the song together and their voices don't so much blend as bolster each other. They grow more disconnected in the final verse, and the dissonance adds a psychedelic flavour. By the end of the song, the fruity organ has become the dominant instrument. This sets the tone for the entire album: late-60s experimental pop mixed with 70s rock swagger, juiced up with go-for-broke garage rock energy.

The goal of the lyrics, said Jack to *Uncut*, was to 'find the beauty in clichéd phrases'. The lyrics are a litany of pat advice, but beneath the surface, there's a cynical take on matrimony: it's about the pressure to get married for the sake of it, even if it costs you your vitality:

> When you have completed what you thought you had to do
> And your blood's depleted to the point of stable glue
> Then you'll get along

Critics have noted this song's musical similarities to Joe Jackson's 1979 new wave banger, 'Is She Really Going Out With Him?'. This song could be read as a companion piece to that song. 'Is She Really...' is written from the perspective of a romantic reject, who is bitter that the object of his affection is stepping out with another man. 'Steady...' could be the other man's story, showing that the grass is not always greener on the other side of the fence.

This was the first single from the album and it reached number 54 on the *Billboard* Hot 100, number one on the Alternative Airplay chart, number four in the UK and number 47 in Australia. This remains the second biggest hit of Jack's career after 'Seven Nation Army', and it is still a highlight of his live shows.

'Hands'

'Hands' is as perfect an example of modern power pop as you could hope to find: all surging power chords, crashing cymbals and loveably unpolished harmonies. It's like a newly unearthed Raspberries song. Benson's straight-faced vocals add an edge to the unabashed romanticism of the lyrics. Like many a great pop song, this uses religious imagery to convey the rapture of being in love. This girl has healing hands; she can help him see the light and she finds the good inside him. When Jack joins in on the chorus, it almost sounds like they're frightened of how in love they are, like they're seeing a Biblically accurate angel. After two verses and choruses, the song slows down to a chug that builds back up slowly with wordless 'oh oh'-ing, before another chorus closes things off in tent revival style. It's the kind of classic pop trick that is designed for live performance.

This was released as the second Raconteurs single. The video, featuring the band playing with deaf teenagers, is quite sweet.

'Broken Boy Soldier'

Jack switches up the tone with this spooky song. The opening feedback sounds like the howl of a doomed spirit, and it turns into an eerie drone that chases the band throughout the song. The combination of overripe acoustic rhythm guitar and sinuous Eastern-sounding electric licks makes it sound as if an Appalachian folk singer has crashed an Indian raga session. The sound is reminiscent of Syd Barrett's solo work, which, by the early 2000s, was the common reference point for lo-fi psychedelic acts like The Flaming Lips and the Elephant 6 collective (Neutral Milk Hotel, The Apples In Stereo, Of Montreal, etc.). The line, 'I'm child and man and child again', and the closing line, 'The boy never gets older', sounds like one of Roger Waters' lyrics from *Wish You Were Here* or *The Wall* about Barrett's mental decline. The lyrics are also Barrett-esque in how Jack puts a twisted spin on childhood memories. Old toy soldiers represent parts of his life he has to leave behind – including ex-friends and enemies. He starts the song asking forgiveness of himself, but by the end, he is determined: 'I'm done ripping myself off'. This is a far cry from the Jack, who wrote dewy-eyed childhood reminisces like 'We're Going To Be Friends'.

This was demoed during the first Raconteur's session and became the second song they wrote together. It was also the album's third single, and it reached number 22 in the UK chart. The music video, directed by Floria Sigismondi, featuring creepy stop-motion toys, is one of Jack's best.

'Intimate Secretary'

This is the second best rock song with 'secretary' in the title – the first being Paul McCartney's demented 'Temporary Secretary'. But this is the first rock song to use the word 'kakistocracy', referring to a social structure where the least qualified people are at the top of the hierarchy. Surely, there's no better word to describe the music industry! But they might be hinting at something deeper with the title and the lyric, 'This fellow's craft is just not for sharing'. The terms 'intimate secretary' and 'fellowcraft' refer to positions within the Freemasons. It seems as if the band are calling out the secret rulers of the world for the terrible job they're doing – the portmanteau 'demockery' is used. But that message is buried under a series of nursery-level rhymes about rabbits and teapots. It's all extremely odd, culminating in the lines:

Then on rubble of scummest malarkey
Down with luck we'll see Ecclesiarchy

That last word refers to a society ruled by religion. Is Jack, the former altar boy, hoping to roll back the separation of church and state? Your guess is as good as mine.

The music is as confused and fascinating as the lyrics. It starts with another intense build-up, as instruments haphazardly scramble to find purchase. Then it explodes into a forceful stop-start arrangement that prevents the listener from ever getting too comfortable. This is one of the best whole-band performances on the album. Jack and Benson alternate singing verse and chorus. Jack plays Hammond organ and Lawrence and Keeler handle the time changes with aplomb. There's so much going on that it feels like this song is over before it has begun.

'Together'

After the frantic feel of the preceding songs, it was a wise decision to ease off and close out side one of the record with a friendly ballad from Benson. This has a simple message about working for happiness rather than merely wishing for it. Benson's delivery is, perhaps, too laconic for the message to feel uplifting, but the music gives the song a warm-hearted feel.

'Level'

This is the most overtly 'Jack-esque' Raconteurs song thus far. It's a simple idea well-executed: Jack's girl is 'on the level' and it frustrates him. He does not know how to deal with a woman who's honest with him, and he's worried he'll trip himself up: 'I can't see the road if I'm lookin' at the signs'. The sea-sawing music contrasts nicely with the title metaphor. Jack's rambunctious guitar solo was apparently written by Benson, a sign that Jack is a dedicated team player.

'Store Bought Bones'

This opens with a big honking Hammond organ riff doubled on guitar. It is a taste of the maximalist musical approach Jack would take on later albums, using keyboards and guitars together for a wall of sound. He would also manipulate his guitar tone more, as previewed here, where he uses so much sustain that it sounds almost like a theremin. Jack and Benson sing this strident song together, calling out people – perhaps Jack's former allies-turned-competitors – who try to 'buy' inspiration from what's popular.

'Yellow Sun'

Here is more sunny power pop from Benson, albeit with strummed acoustic guitar and electric piano instead of power chords; Keeler's relentless drumming gives it propulsive energy, nonetheless. Benson sings the first three verses, wherein the shining sun symbolises his confidence at scoring with a girl, but then Jack takes over for the bittersweet final verse, where the protagonist realises that he has been played. These vocals, harmonies included, were recorded on the first take. That is pretty impressive, even if this is the album's least musically and lyrically interesting song.

'Call It A Day'

The title might seem like a strange sentiment for the penultimate song on a band's first album! But this is a straightforward break-up song, albeit an unusually relaxed one. Benson sounds resigned to his fate, relieved that he has an excuse to end things. But there is a twist in the final verse, where it seems as if he's threatening to harm himself in revenge for her manipulations:

> But I stake my life
> And I'll swear by this knife
> That it's all by your design

The nasal backing vocals almost feel like they're mocking the narrator, which adds a frisson to this otherwise lethargic song.

'Blue Veins'

For the first time, Jack ends an album with one of its strongest songs. This claustrophobic slow blues is a world away from the sunny singalong of 'Steady, As She Goes', so naturally, it became a cult favourite amongst his fans. It opens with backwards tape, like Jimi Hendrix's 'Are You Experienced?' (another all-time great album closer), and the whole song is steeped in a dark psychedelic ambience. It has a similar feel to U2's 'Love Is Blindness', the closer of that band's own cross-genre song cycle, *Achtung Baby*. Both songs have the same 'late night, inner city, last call' feel. Jack may have been inspired by 'Love Is Blindness' because he covered it (see 'Non-Album Tracks, B-Sides And Rarities').

But while that U2 song seethes with hurt feelings, 'Blue Veins' is a grateful ode to a supportive woman. It doesn't sound that way, though, which is perhaps why fans latched onto it. Love is complicated, after all, especially when the most obvious interpretation of this song is that it's about Meg. Consider the opening verse:

> When I was surrounded by the world
> You were the only one who came
> And you were the only one astounded
> Which kept me grounded
> As the other girls trashed my very name

Jack has always said that Meg was the glue holding The White Stripes together, and the one who could puncture his arrogance when he needed it. If 'Blue Veins' is, indeed, a tribute to her, then it came at an opportune time, given what happened after their next album...

Icky Thump (2007)

Personnel:
Jack White: vocals, guitar, mandolin, keyboards, synthesisers
Meg White: drums, percussion, vocals
With:
Regulo Aldama: trumpet
Jim Drury: Scottish smallpipes
Producer: Jack White
Recorded at Blackbird, Nashville, Tennessee, February 2007
Release date: 15 June 2007
Chart places: US: 2, UK: 1, Aus: 3
All tracks written by Jack White, except where noted

The final White Stripes album was not intended as such. At the time, it seemed like the natural next step on Jack's artistic path. It retained the experimental edge of *Get Behind Me Satan*, but ditched the weirdness for weirdness' sake, and added some of the pop power that made *Broken Boy Soldiers* so likeable. It does not sound like a grand final statement. In fact, it sounds harder and heavier than any other White Stripes album, as if the band were readying to play big arena rock shows. This was Jack's first album recorded in his new home of Nashville. In classic rock 'n' roll fashion, Jack grew tired of his hometown and the backbiting there, so in 2007, he sold his old family home and severed ties with Detroit. 'The story of the city of Detroit became our authenticity, that dirty, crumbling town', he said to *Uncut*. 'I don't see a lot of other artists getting asked about where they live, but I get asked about where I live constantly'. So moving to Nashville provided some relief: 'It's all country, so half of them don't care about me, which is great'. In 2018, he said to *Mojo*: 'Nashville reinvigorated everything I did. There were no hipsters about. It was a clean slate'.

Jack's other projects meant that they started recording this album with few complete songs, so this album was mostly written in the studio. He became infatuated with editing and splicing the songs together without using a computer. As a result, this took the longest time to record for any White Stripes album: a whopping three weeks. This album was arguably the most 'hands-on' Meg ever got with production. She wanted a different drum feel for this album, and she used editing to 'punch in' the drums.

The album's title comes from a phrase Jack heard Karen Elson use. Presumably, being British, she was referring to the ancient, secret, Lancashire martial art known as 'Ecky Thump' – as portrayed in the 1975 *The Goodies* episode 'Kung Fu Capers'. This episode is infamous for being the cause of one of the few recorded cases of someone laughing himself to death! The cover sees Jack and Meg dressed like stereotypical Cockney 'pearly queens', a further expression of Jack's Anglophilia. However, many of the songs are infused with explicitly American sentiments and imagery.

So, consider this album the ultimate synthesis of Jack's duelling pommy and Yankee influences.

As well as CD and vinyl, this album was released on USB: 3333 copies, each of flash drives designed to look like Jack or Meg, containing Apple audio files. They supported the album with a tour where Jack wanted to play every province and territory of Canada. The tour was filmed for the documentary *Under Great White Northern Lights*. This documentary became an epitaph when it was announced that Meg was suffering from anxiety, and they ceased live performances. After Elson gave birth to Jack's second child, it seemed like a signal to take a break. 'I had a baby coming, my son was being born, so we didn't have a lot of time left. We were trying to cram everything into a short time span, and we were just plowin', man!' he said to *Music Radar*.

> We were playing two shows a day in Canada, then we'd fly to France and do a TV show there, then we were back in England on tour, and we were just killin' it, man. The train was out of control. I just came from a Raconteurs tour and went right into that, so I was already full-speed. Meg had come from a dead halt for a year and went right back into that madness. Meg is a very shy girl, a very quiet and shy person. To go full speed from a dead halt is overwhelming, and we had to take a break.

Ultimately, Jack and Meg decided to end the band entirely. Their performance of 'We're Going To Be Friends' for Conan O'Brien on his last episode of *Late Night* on 20 February 2009 was their last performance as a duo. The White Stripes confirmed their split in 2011, citing that they wanted 'to preserve what is beautiful and special about the band'.

'Icky Thump'

This is The White Stripes' final 24-carat masterpiece. It remains in Jack's solo setlists and is guaranteed to get the audience headbanging every time. A pounding two-note riff kicks off the lengthy introduction, where, over a grinding beat, Jack plays a 1959 Univox clavioline – an electric keyboard with a thick, fuzzy tone. Pop fans might know the instrument from The Beatles' B-side 'Baby, You're A Rich Man', where it sounds like a snake charmer. In Jack's hands, it sounds more like a heavy metal oboe. As the song goes on, Jack's Univox playing gets more unrestrained until it seems like the song is glitching. There is also a guitar solo that sounds as if it's being squeezed out bar by bar. Indeed, both the instrumental bridge and the guitar solo were cut up and spliced in piecemeal. There is also no chorus, just a pile-driving riff.

Just as striking as the music are the lyrics. They tell the story of a drunken fool who stumbles into Mexico looking for a good time, gets waylaid by a sexy señorita (a redhead, of course) and wakes up handcuffed to the bed with his money stolen. So far, so typical for a raunchy American comedy movie. But most listeners focus on the first few lines of the third verse:

White Americans, what? Nothing better to do
Why don't you kick yourself out? You're an immigrant too
Who's using who? What should we do?
Well, you can't be a pimp and a prostitute too

These lyrics were interpreted as a comment on George W. Bush's hardline anti-immigration policies. The first two lines have a clear meaning, but the other two are more ambiguous. I interpret them as calling out Americans who panic over illegal immigrants 'stealing' jobs, yet look the other way when they are exploited for cheap labour. The music video includes Spanish subtitles to sharpen the political edge.

Jack waited a long time to make any obvious socio-political statement in his music. In fact, he told John Harris in *Q* that he purposefully 'stopped myself having an opinion about politics and opening my mouth about it'. And really, these lines stick out like a sore thumb in the context of the song as a whole. One could read them as something spoken by the woman in the song to the protagonist – calling him out as an ugly American coming to Mexico for cheap thrills. So, this isn't necessarily Jack speaking his own political views; it's, once again, him playing a character.

Any controversy the lyrics might have generated did not affect the song's reception. It was the first single from this album, and it reached number 26 on the US *Billboard* Hot 100 – making it the group's only mainstream chart hit. It also reached number two on the UK singles chart, which was their highest placing in that country. For the first time, a significant portion of the band's sales came from downloads, with iTunes having established itself among young people as the way to access new music.

In 2016, Jack suffered a problem faced by many musicians: a politician using one of their songs in a campaign. In this case, it was Donald Trump, who used 'Seven Nation Army'. Jack objected, and, in response, released a t-shirt with the slogan 'Icky Trump' on the front and the above lyrics on the back.

'You Don't Know What Love Is (You Just Do As You're Told)'
Time for some tough love! In this hard-hitting song, Jack tries his hand at motivational speaking, urging a woman in a bad relationship to stand up for herself. This song was written while The Raconteurs toured with Bob Dylan, and there are shades of his 'Just Like A Woman' – notably, the condescending tone. While Jack recognises the woman's own agency – 'You're not hopeless, or helpless' – and he acknowledges how blunt he's being – 'I hate to sound cold' – he's not going to let her give up on herself – 'Until you say you deserve better, I'm gonna lay right into you'. This is arguably the bluntest he's ever been, and if this song was directed at someone in particular, you have to hope they got the message.

While the musical arrangement is unmistakably The White Stripes – all ringing power chords and crashing cymbals – the sound is bigger and the production glossier. The guitar riff is also shadowed by keyboards throughout. Meg is almost drowned out, as the guitar acts like percussion. This is the post-Raconteurs Jack fully unleashed, no longer determined to stick to the basic lo-fi White Stripes model, even on a classic White Stripes-style song. This was the album's second single.

'300 M.P.H. Torrential Outpour Blues'

This is the second-longest White Stripes song, a whopping five and a half minutes. It doesn't quite justify its length, but it's still a good listen. Jack's goal was to cover as many different kinds of blues music as he could, from introspective folk blues to explosive blues rawk. The way the gentle verses explode into overdriven guitar wailing is reminiscent of early Led Zeppelin, ala 'Babe I'm Gonna Leave You'. This is also one of Meg's greatest showcases. She used two drum kits and they sound digitally adjusted to give them more of a 'thump'.

Again, Jack tells off a girl for not behaving right, and again, this is rooted in his insecurity: 'There's three people in the mirror, and I'm wondering which of them I should choose'. Best of all is the final line, which harkens back to old-fashioned Robert Johnson-style fatalism: 'In that graveyard, I'm gonna have the shiniest pair of shoes'.

'Conquest' (Corky Robbins)

Here, we see Jack's crate-digging instincts pay off. This is a cover of a Patti Page song that was almost lost to time and was, thus, ripe for reinvention. The White Stripes' faux-mariachi arrangement is similar to the original, but everything is cranked to eleven. There is many a musical delight, from the opening fanfare to the massed vocal interjections. The battle between Jack's guitar and Regulo Aldama's trumpet is especially fun. Jack is also on fine vocal form, camping it up to telenovela levels. It is a classic 'battle of the sexes' song, where the pursued gets the upper hand on the pursuer, ala Smokey Robinson's 'The Hunter Gets Captured By The Game'.

This was the third single from the album, released on various formats, including three different coloured 7" vinyl records. It reached number 30 on the Alternative Airplay chart. A Spanish language version of this song – retitled 'Conquesta' – became the final White Stripes single in January 2008 (see 'Non-Album Tracks, B-Sides And Rarities').

'Bone Broke'

Back to basics now, with a primal two-chord riff that's so rudimentary, it feels incomplete. It feels as if the song is continuously getting started. Jack calls out a rich girl for not recognising her privilege while he works at the liquor store. The whole 'rich girl-poor boy' dynamic has been done to death in pop music, and this song doesn't really add anything to the conversation.

'Prickly Thorn, But Sweetly Worn'

The album's most extreme departure is this excursion into full-blown Celtic folk territory. This was a tribute to Jack's recently deceased father, who died in 2006, and was dedicated to 'Good Guy Gorm'. Gorm's ancestry was Scottish by way of Nova Scotia, hence the mandolin and pipes. In the short list of rock songs featuring bagpipes, this ranks around the top of the middle. (Number one, of course, being 'It's A Long Way To The Top' by AC/DC).

This is a welcome change of pace after five tracks of bluff and bluster. The chorus is a wordless 'Li de di' singalong, akin to a sea shanty. The remaining lyrics reference silver birches and thistles, evoking the Scottish highlands of the imagination. This segues into...

'St. Andrew (This Battle Is In The Air)'

...a disorienting collage of backwards percussion, sped-up pipes, shrill guitar and spoken word from Meg. Jack's Catholic upbringing shows through in the reference to Andrew, the patron saint of Scotland. Meg plays the role of a recently deceased soul wandering the afterlife, looking for heaven. The placement of this song after Jack's tribute to his father paints a bleak picture.

'Little Cream Soda'

This song has a sinister surf music vibe, with a galloping rhythm, pushed along by shrill guitar interjections. Jack had fallen in love with this particular guitar tone, and it became integral to his sound from here on. Jack speaks rather than sings the lyrics, and the effect is like a sped-up 'talking blues'. He laments the complications of his life and reminisces about a simpler time. It's as if he didn't heed his own advice in 'Little Room':

Now my mind is filled with rubber tires and forest fires
And whether I'm a liar
And lots of other situations where I don't know what to do

'Rag And Bone'

This song harkens back to the childlike role-play of early White Stripes. Jack and Meg play 'rag and bone' collectors, 'rag and bone' being a British term for people who collect scraps of cloth, paper, metal and other things that could be sold for reuse. Over the stuttering opening riff, Jack hams it up like a carnival barker, excitingly relating to Meg all the sellable stuff they've found in some abandoned house. Jack gradually gets himself so worked up that he breaks into song. For her part, hilariously, Meg just hums enthusiastically.

This song is one of Jack's least subtle metaphors. His entire career has been about taking the forgotten and undervalued parts of American musical history and reupholstering them for modern audiences. 'You take things that other people aren't noticing and make something beautiful out of them, keeping them alive', he told *The Sun*. Thus, it is appropriate that this song is one of his most indebted to the 12-bar blues style, with some Jack-like stop-start flourishes.

This was technically the second single from the album, as a free flexi-disc given away with 120,000 copies of the *NME* issue from 6 June 2007. So, this song's release involved reviving an outdated format; how very meta.

'I'm Slowly Turning Into You'
Musically, this is by-the-numbers rock, with the best moment being the pre-chorus, where Meg's whispered vocals create a claustrophobic paranoid feel as if we've been made privy to Jack's intrusive thoughts. Lyrically, it is about having to adjust your behaviour to match the person you live with, and how frustrating that can be. Jack said to *Mojo*: 'When someone comes into your life, you have to decide: which 'you' are you going to give them? A lot of times in bad relationships, you give them the fake version and that's why it doesn't end up working out'.

But the song ends with a positive twist:

That was the mirror
It made everything clearer
...
And it might sound a little strange for me to say to you
But I'm proud to be you

So, he is turning into ... himself? Yes, this song is Jack realising that he is proud of the person he has become. Or rather, he is happy to play the role of 'Jack White', his fabricated rock star persona. He goes from saying, 'I like to keep my little shell intact' to 'I even love it when you're faking it'.

'A Martyr For My Love For You'
This assuming song has the strongest melody on the album. It rides in on waves of cymbals and a gothic organ fanfare, before settling into a tight, almost hip-hop groove, with Jack near rapping the lyrics. He tells the tragicomic story of a teenage neurotic, who finds the perfect girl on a trip to the zoo, but backs away because he is certain he'll sabotage himself: 'I could stay a while, but sooner or later I'll break your smile'. It's those intrusive thoughts again.

'Catch Hell Blues'
As the title implies, this is the most pure 'blues' song on the album, complete with 'fire and brimstone' imagery, as Jack warns the listener against looking for trouble. It's not a great song, but it is a great guitar showcase. The lengthy slide introduction is particularly cool, while the riff after the first verse sounds like it was designed to startle dogs.

'Effect And Cause'

It would be nice to report that The White Stripes signed off with an epic song that consolidated everything that made them exceptional into one grand statement, ala The Beatles' *Abbey Road* medley. But no one knew this would be their last will and testament, and so they signed off with another jaunty little acoustic ditty. Meg barely features, unfortunately, but Jack's skills as a tunesmith are in full effect.

This is (sigh) another song calling out a woman, but at least this time, it's fun. This song is directly autobiographical, said Jack to *Q*. It is about a woman he loved long ago, whose problem was that when Jack reacted to the trouble she caused, she blamed him for it – putting the 'effect' before the 'cause'. Jack compares this to various illogical ideas, such as blaming a baby for its mother getting pregnant or the hearse for a person dying. It sounds trite on paper, but it's performed with such conviction that the overall effect is charming.

And with this, we bid adieu to The White Stripes, for the foreseeable future at least.

Consolers Of The Lonely (2008)

Personnel:
Brendan Benson: vocals, guitar, organ, piano
Patrick Keeler: drums, percussion
Jack Lawrence: bass guitar, banjo, backing vocals
Jack White: vocals, guitar, stylophone, piano, organ
With:
Dean Fertita: clavinet
Dirk Powell: strings
The Memphis Horns: horns
Flory Dory Girls: backing vocals
Producer: Brendan Benson & Jack White
Recorded at Blackbird, Nashville, Tennessee, April 2007 and February 2008
Release date: 25 March 2008
Chart places: US: 7, UK: 8, Aus: 18
All tracks written by Brendan Benson and Jack White, except where noted

The second Raconteurs album arrived less than a year after the final White
Stripes album, signalling that, despite his first band breaking up, Jack was not
planning on stopping or even slowing down. But this album was not written
and recorded with the Stripes' break-up hanging over the band; it was begun
in between *Icky Thump* being mixed and The White Stripes going on tour,
and then finished in a three-week burst.

Despite this tight turnaround, *Consolers Of The Lonely* sounds nothing
like a rush job. If their debut was a throwback to 1960s freakbeat, their
sophomore album plays like a souped-up 1970s Laurel Canyon album. There
are elements of folk rock, country, power pop, psychedelia and art rock, and
everything is cranked to 11. It is as if the band felt that they needed to get
everything they had to say down on wax before their conflicting schedules
pulled them apart. The fact that it took 12 years for them to follow this up
speaks to that sense of do-or-die. Jack, in particular, sounds like he has
something to prove. 'I can play guitar solos that I can't in The White Stripes',
he said to Swiss journalist Hanspeter Kuenzler.

This album was recorded in Blackbird Studio in Nashville, where they
were influenced by Nashville's storied history as the home of country music.
They had all manner of vintage instruments and equipment available to
use, and use them they did. The 'old-timey' vibe was also expressed on the
cover, which shows the band looking like the warm-up act for a medicine
show. This photo was shot using vintage tintype technology – only the most
outdated and inconvenient would do for Jack!

The band rush-released this album, just over a month after they finished
recording it, with no prior announcement, no advertising campaign, no teaser
singles and no warm-up gigs. This was an effort to bypass the usual tiresome
promotional obligations, but it wound up backfiring on the band. Radiohead

Above: He's got the blues: Jack White rockin' his current blue & black aesthetic. (*Alamy*)

Left: The White Stripes' original red, black & white aesthetic is in full display on their self-titled debut album. (*Sympathy For The Record Industry*)

Right: Pretentious? Moi? *De Stijl* is The White Stripes in fine style. (*Sympathy For The Record Industry*)

Left: Get your blood pumping with The White Stripes' era-defining third album *White Blood Cells*. (*Sympathy For The Record Industry*)

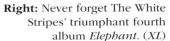

Right: Never forget The White Stripes' triumphant fourth album *Elephant*. (*XL*)

Left: A note for collectors: The US vinyl version of *Elephant* has Meg wearing widow's black, while the rest of the world has her in ghostly white. (*XL*)

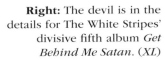

Right: The devil is in the details for The White Stripes' divisive fifth album *Get Behind Me Satan*. (*XL*)

Left: Jack serenades a nonplussed Meg in the video for 'The Hardest Button To Button'.

Right: Even while recovering from a busted hand (see the cast), Jack can still shred.

Left: Get the point? The video for 'Seven Nation Army' sold the two-piece as a world-conquering force.

Right: Totally wired: the video for 'Black Math' helped sell Jack as the mad scientist of modern rock.

Left: Jack and Meg see red in the clip for 'Icky Thump'.

Right: The Mexico-set video for 'Icky Thump' was The White Stripes' one foray into overt political commentary.

Left: Like Dave Davies and Moe Tucker, Meg's rare turns on the mic were enough to leave you wanting more. (*Jon Super/ Getty*)

Right: Meg singing 'Passive Manipulation'. They're a confident band that can bring out the kettle drums for a 50-second song! (*Alamy*)

Right: As Jack's look went from skinny indie kid to swashbuckling witchdoctor, Meg blessedly stayed the same. (*Tabatha Fireman/Getty*)

Left: A beautiful and bittersweet shot from the *Under Great White Northern Light* film. (*Three Foot Giant/ Woodshed Films*)

Left: Put up your dukes: The Raconteurs come out fighting on their debut *Broken Boy Soldiers*. (*XL*)

Right: 'ave a butcher's at The White Stripes in 'pearly queen' gear on the cover of their sixth and final album *Icky Thump*. (*XL*)

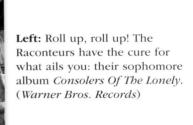

Left: Roll up, roll up! The Raconteurs have the cure for what ails you: their sophomore album *Consolers Of The Lonely*. (*Warner Bros. Records*)

Right: In retrospect, it feels like the covers for the first two Dead Weather albums were trying to hide Jack's involvement. Their debut features Alison Mosshart only. (*Warner Bros. Records*)

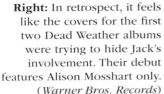

Left: The ritual is about to begin! Take a dip in *Sea Of Cowards*, The Dead Weather's second album. (*Warner Bros. Records*)

Right: Vulture culture: Jack debuts his sombre new colour scheme on his debut solo album *Blunderbuss*. (*Third Man*)

Left: It's lonely at the top: Jack takes stock of his life and career on his second solo album *Lazaretto*. (*Third Man*)

Right: The Dead Weather look like road warriors facing down the apocalypse on the cover of their underrated third album *Dodge And Burn*. (*Third Man*)

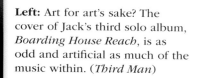

Left: Art for art's sake? The cover of Jack's third solo album, *Boarding House Reach*, is as odd and artificial as much of the music within. (*Third Man*)

Right: Give a big hand for The Raconteurs' long-delayed third album *Help Us Stranger*. (*Third Man*)

Left: The dark and disquieting cover of Jack's fourth solo album, *Fear Of The Dawn*, does not reflect the wild sounds within. (*Third Man*)

Right: Dream Weaver: despite coming hot on the heels of his fourth, Jack's fifth solo album, *Entering Heaven Alive*, is a finely crafted piece of work. (*Third Man*)

Left: Jack duets with himself in the video clip for 'I'm Shakin". Hey, the man likes to work with the best.

Right: Another Blues Brothers sequel? No, it's a dapper Jack White performing 'I'm Shakin".

Left: Your guess is as good as mine as to what's going on in the video for 'Over And Over And Over'.

Right: Scenes like this from the video for 'Over And Over And Over' make me suspect that Jack feels a trifle self-conscious at times. He should write a song or 20 about that …

Left: It feels like there's an army of Jack's comin' at ya in the video for 'Fear Of The Dawn'.

Right: Jack plays The Man With No Name… or Pigment, in the video for 'If I Die Tomorrow'.

Above: The boys are back in town: Jack playing live with The Raconteurs. (*Carlos Gonzalez/Star Tribune/Getty*)

Below: Jack returned to his first instrument, the drums, to play live with The Dead Weather. (*Ebet Roberts/Getty*)

Above: I took these two photos during Jack's concert at the Harvest Rock Festival in Adelaide 2022. (*Ben L. Connor*)

Right: Take a bow, Jack, after one of the most breathless, chaotic and fun shows I've ever attended. (*Ben L. Connor*)

Left: The White Stripes' first live album, *Under Great White Northern Lights,* holds a special place in many fans' hearts as a record of their final tour. (*Third Man*)

Right: Rev it up with The White Stripes' *Greatest Hits* – banger after banger after banger. (*Third Man*)

Left: Or, if you prefer to get mellow, *Acoustic Recordings 1998-2016* shows how Jack can do more with less. (*Third Man*)

and Marillion had previously released surprise albums online for free, and in those cases, the novelty helped promote the album. Those bands also relied on their passionate long-term fanbases to spread the word. The problem for The Raconteurs was that they did not have a big enough pop culture profile, so this album came and went with only the hardcore faithful hearing it.

But time has told its own story, and now fans say that this album surpasses The Raconteurs' debut. Again, my opinion departs from the general consensus, as the debut has a freshness and lightness that I find more endearing. But even I have to admit that this album feels more like a major work from a band with a unified purpose. I do think the album is overlong, and some songs could have been cut to make for a punchier listening experience. But I doubt any fans could agree on which songs to cut!

'Consoler Of The Lonely'
The album opens with the sound of laughter, and you can faintly hear a child say, 'Daddy, will you tell me the story about the chickens again?' The song then abruptly takes off, as if the band just noticed that they were on the clock. This has a stop-start arrangement, with stomping verses sung by Benson, and Jack singing the slower bridge, followed by an instrumental outro.

Lyrically, this is an odd way to start an album. Benson paints a depressing picture of an isolated and bored man, and – despite the song's title – Jack offers little in the way of consolation:

If you're looking for an accomplice
A confederate, somebody's who's helpless
You're gonna find, you'll find yourself alone

This song's message is that you can't rely on other people to lift your spirits – you must do it yourself, as these boys do by rocking out together.

'Salute Your Solution'
The album continues its solipsistic theme with this song about the need to take care of oneself when other people are dumping their problems on you. With its fearsome two-chord riff, breathless vocals and shrill guitar solo, this song sounds like it could have been included on *Icky Thump*. At the time, it seemed to me like a mistake for the album's flagship single to sound so similar to Jack's previous band. This was an opportunity for the band to stake out new sonic territories, rather than rehash past glories. But I was mistaken, for the single reached number four on the Alternative Airplay chart, making it the band's second most successful single.

'You Don't Understand Me'
As the title indicates, this is another self-involved song. This one is about the inability of people to truly know one another. The line, 'In the court of my

heart your ignorance is treason', is suggestive of the way narcissists take tiny miscommunications as massive personal slights. But despite the occasionally eye-roll-inducing lyrics, this is a very pretty song. It is also a good example of The Raconteurs' knack for genre-fusion. The melody rides a gentle piano figure reminiscent of Warren Zevon's less acerbic songs, while subtle washes of horns add a soulful flavour. The harmonies in the bridge have a Beatles-esque tone, while the finale, with Jack hammering the piano louder and louder before the song fades away to a gentle wisp, is as theatrical as glam rock.

'Old Enough'
Just as the album seemed a little po-faced, this song brings the good vibes. This is a near-perfect country rock pastiche, complete with a hoedown fiddle riff. The production perfectly balances the electric and acoustic elements, and for the first time on the album, it feels like the music can fully breathe. The breakdown going into the bridge is particularly juicy, with the instruments all coming together on a killer riff. Then, the bridge is followed by a delicious acoustic flourish.

Benson sings lead on the first few verses, while Jack takes the final verse, and their voices converge in harmony throughout. I would not be surprised if Jack was the lead songwriter, considering that this is yet another song calling out a naive woman. She is not 'old enough' to realise that she does not have to maintain a tough facade. There's more sympathy than cynicism in this depiction, as evidenced in the best lines:

And how have you gotten by so far
Without having no visible scar?
No one knowing who you really are

This was the third single from the album, and it deserved more success. It was too country (read: cornball) for any lingering 'rock revival' fans, too far outside the mainstream for country fans and too far from the cutting edge – which in 2008 was preppy neo-yacht rock like Vampire Weekend and Grizzly Bear – for indie fans. The band doubled down on the country elements with a re-recording that is substantially different (see 'Non-Album Tracks, B-Sides And Rarities').

'The Switch And The Spur'
Howdy pard'ner! The gang saddle up for a Wild West adventure on this song, which sounds like Ennio Morricone was forced at gunpoint to add Hollywood pomp to an otherwise unremarkable song. It opens with a most dramatic flourish: piano doubled up by mariachi horns. That then leads into an intense story about a poisoned outlaw lost in the desert, who swears revenge. There is another herky-jerky guitar solo from Jack and an apocalyptic ending, with Benson calling down God's wrath on any who 'trespass against us.'

'Hold Up'

This hard-rocking song is the weakest on the album. It has a simplistic hook and the barest hint of melody, with only the excessive use of the wah-wah pedal to distinguish it. In keeping with the Wild West theme of the preceding song, the title is a pun on a robbery 'hold up' and being 'holed up' in a cell. Jack once again vents his spleen at the modern world:

> Had enough of these modern times
> About to drive me out of my mind
> And you know this too well
> I'm holed up in my little cell

'Top Yourself'

This song starts out acoustic, then revs up into a slide-guitar-driven groove that sounds similar to early Faces, or, more recently, Ben Harper (an undersung figure in the modern blues rock scene, in my opinion). There is also banjo, although this is mixed quite low. All up, this is a pleasant song that never fully catches fire.

This is another title with a double meaning. 'Top yourself' is a euphemism for suicide, and we hope that Jack is not taunting a girl for contemplating that!

> How you gonna top yourself
> When there is nobody else?
> How you gonna do it by yourself?
> 'Cause I'm not gonna be here to help you

My less stressful interpretation is that 'top' refers to being the 'top dog' in the relationship: the girl in question needs a man to boss her around, and Jack has recently vacated the position, leaving her adrift:

> See you've been getting it all for free
> Guess you better get yourself a sugar daddy

So yes, it is another song about a toxic relationship, with an unbalanced power dynamic. Might as well ask the Red Hot Chili Peppers to stop writing songs about California.

'Many Shades Of Black'

This bombastic break-up song is a highlight of the album. While, like many songs on this album, it feels pieced together from half-finished snatches, the band's full-bore performance and the kitchen-sink production overwhelm any doubts. The violent acoustic opening riff gives way to a horn fanfare before the song settles into a finger-snapping blues groove. A paint-stripping guitar solo from Jack seals the deal. This was correctly issued as a single, but likely reached more ears via a cover by neo-soul singer and XL labelmate Adele (see 'Non-Album Tracks, B-Sides And Rarities').

'Five On The Five'

This is another hard-and-fast Jack-led song, but closer to Foo Fighters than to The White Stripes. It is the definition of dumb fun, with a fantastic bass-led breakdown leading into the final chorus. Jack seems upbeat that he's found a girl he is simpatico with – 'The day you found me, girl, my laugh became stereo' – but he's worried that she is only attracted to the celebrity version of him – 'Yeah, I look nothing like the kids in the videos'. As to what 'five on the five' refers to, some have suggested it refers to driving or gambling, but your guess is as good as mine.

'Attention'

Here is another hard rock song, like The Black Keys, by way of, well, Foo Fighters again. There is a big honking organ line, but the chorus riff, with its galloping drums, comes straight out of the Dave Grohl playbook. The middle eight, with its heavier guitar tone, talk box-style effects and yelping backing vocals, seems to come from another song entirely. As with a few songs on this album, the whole is less than the sum of the parts.

'Pull This Blanket Off'

This is a short piano-led song from Jack, with bluesy guitar flourishes. The lyrics are abstract, but generally suggest frustration, perhaps with the way he is seen as this humourless, autocratic figure due to his eccentric self-discipline:

> It's hard sticking to your guns
> When everybody's having fun

'Rich Kid Blues' (Terry Reid)

This is a cover of a song by British singer-guitarist Terry Reid from his 1969 self-titled record. The lyrics – a jumble of blues cliches – work as a sardonic comment on Jack's status as the world's wealthier blues purist. This is a well-executed cover but could have been relegated to a B-side to make this album snappier. However, if it gets people to check out Terry Reid, then no harm done. Fans of this cover should check out the 1969 album or 1976's *Seed Of Memory*.

'These Stones Will Shout'

Another semi-acoustic song, this could have been sequenced between 'Five On The Five' and 'Attention' to vary the pace a little. Tucked away near the end of this album, it feels like an afterthought. The lyrics, once again imploring a woman to speak up for herself, are nothing to write home about. The music is more interesting: the switch from acoustic to electric is adroitly handled, and it includes what sounds like a celeste or some vibes very low in the mix.

'Carolina Drama'

Thus far, *Consolers* ... has demonstrated The Raconteurs' chemistry as a band, as well as Jack and Benson's ability to switch genres between, and sometimes during, songs. What it has not done is give us an irrefutable Jack White masterpiece. So, for Jack fans more interested in his quirky songwriting voice than his guitar skills, 'Carolina Drama' was a real gift.

The acoustic guitar and country fiddle place this firmly in the 'story song' idiom. Jack was inspired by Bob Dylan epics, such as 'Isis' and 'Lily, Rosemary And The Jack Of Hearts', but this lacks those songs' easy-going vibe. It is more in tune with the long-standing folk tradition of murder ballads. It combines the claustrophobic paranoia of Neil Young's 'Powderfinger' with the steady-building intensity of Led Zeppelin's 'Gallows Pole'. The result is a Southern Gothic melodrama condensed into a song.

The lyrics are more detailed than Jack's past story songs, but the story is fairly simple. A boy named Billy lives with his mother (a redhead, naturally), his younger brother and his mother's drunken brute of a boyfriend. One day, Billy wakes up and sees the boyfriend attacking a priest, whom Billy assumes must be his long-lost father. Billy clubs the boyfriend to death with a newly delivered bottle of milk. As the family prepares to bury the body and flee the scene, the little brother runs in holding the milkman's hat and a gin bottle. Jack ends the story ambiguously, with a lingering question:

But you wanna know how it ends?
If you must know the truth about the tale
Go and ask the milkman

Is the implication that the younger brother killed the milkman, who witnessed Billy's crime? But if so, would the milkman still be around for us to ask? Are we even supposed to interpret this tale literally? Is this a *Suddenly, Last Summer* situation, to cite one of Tennessee Williams' most overripe psychodramas? (Tennessee being, of course, where the family intends to flee). Jack said to *Vulture* in 2022: 'People are always saying, "Well, who is the milkman? Why does he know the answer to the story?" That's a question I get often. And I'll never tell'.

The climactic wordless singalong is a cathartic release after an intense 55 minutes of Americana bouillabaisse. This song immediately became a fan favourite and a live showcase.

Horehound (2009)

Personnel:
Dean Fertita: guitar, organ, piano, synthesiser
Jack Lawrence: bass, backing vocals, drums, guitar
Alison Mosshart: vocals, guitar, percussion
Jack White: drums, vocals, acoustic guitar
Producer: Jack White
Recorded at Third Man Studio, Nashville, Tennessee, January 2009
Release date: 14 July 2009
Chart places: US: 6, UK: 14, Aus: 48

It would be a long time before The Raconteurs were able to reconvene in the studio, but Jack did not let that stop him from making new music – with a new band. But first, he had to contend with the small matter of becoming a record company mogul.

That Jack owned the rights to his own music and only used the major labels for distribution meant that he, rather than faceless record company suits, reaped the rewards of his hard work. He pocketed a greater slice of the money made from his music than many artists who sold more units. Jack funnelled some of that money into turning his imprint Third Man Records into a proper independent record label. He co-founded the label with Soledad Brothers drummer Ben Swank and Dirtbombs drummer Ben Blackwell. It began as a means for Jack to reissue classic White Stripes singles on vinyl and gradually ballooned into a multipurpose facility in Nashville.

The Third Man Records storefront opened on 11 March 2009, and over the next decade, it became a thriving business enterprise and cultural hotspot. A key draw for Third Man Records, as a store and as a studio, is Jack's emphasis on preserving classic forms of physical media production and distribution. The store includes a wooden vinyl listening booth, a vintage 1960s Scopitone video jukebox loaded with modern music clips, and a 1940s Voice-o-Graph recording and phonograph production machine. There is also a photo studio, a darkroom and a rehearsal space that became a live venue – The Blue Room. Bands play there at a loss to the company, which they make up by selling exclusive live recordings.

Most notably, Third Man Records led the charge for the ongoing vinyl revival. The label's motto was 'Your turntable's not dead'. Jack said to *The Guardian*: 'I want to be a part of the resurgence of things that are tangible, beautiful and soulful, rather than just give in to the digital age'. He began this push at the right time, for in a few years, streaming overtook physical media and became the new dominant music distribution model. Streaming encourages listeners to think of music as a service that can be turned on and off as easily as a faucet. Jack became a leader in the fight against this kind of thinking, starting with promoting vinyl, not just as a collectable or an audiophile obsession, but as a way to own something that the artist put care and attention into making. This included releasing records with all kinds of collectable gimmicks and innovations.

But that was all in the future. On his way to help revitalise the music industry, Jack fell backwards into another band. In October 2008, he decided to record something to break in his new studio. Staying with him at the time was Dean Fertita, another long-time musical associate who contributed clavinet to *Consolers Of The Lonely*. Currently, he was best known as a member of stoner rock icons Queens Of The Stone Age. Jack invited Fertita to play guitar and keyboards, while Jack Lawrence played bass, and Jack returned to his first instrument: the drums.

The final member of the band was Alison Mosshart of The Kills, a two-piece formed in 2001 with English guitarist Jamie Hince. They were initially an even more stripped-down garage rock act than The White Stripes were, with only guitars, a drum machine and Mosshart's voice. Their breakthrough album, 2005's *No Wow*, updated the minimalist post-punk of Young Marble Giants for the post-grunge era, and presaged the genteel alt-pop of The xx. The Kills supported The Raconteurs in 2008, and one night, when Jack lost his voice, Mosshart stepped in to sing two songs. She was in Nashville as Jack was prepping this new music, and he invited her to add vocals.

The foursome quickly gelled as a band. Jack was particularly enthused about combining a male and a female voice the way iconic alt-rock acts like Sonic Youth and Pixies did. The initial goal was to record a one-off 7" single, but they kept going until they had a full album, writing as they recorded.

Horehound was a departure for Jack. For one thing, he did not have a hand in writing every song. Neither did he play the lead instrument nor sing on every track. For the first time as a full member of a band, he was not the focus of attention. The Dead Weather is also sonically different from his other bands. Fertita's keyboards are often the dominant instrument, and the songs are also less riff-based and more groovy. But the grooves are not slick like a dancefloor filler; they're thick like a riptide. Jack's drumming is less about providing rhythm and more about creating atmosphere. The music has a murky swamp-rock feel, as if you're playing a Creedence Clearwater Revival LP at the wrong speed or as if Nick Cave & The Bad Seeds crashed the recording of Bob Dylan's *Time Out Of Mind*.

The Dead Weather were the first live band to perform in the Blue Room when Third Man Records opened, and they went on a 60-date tour through the US and Europe. This album charted higher in the US than the UK, an inverse of usual rankings. Reception to this album was mixed. People generally liked the idea of the band and wanted to love the album. But the consensus was that the songs just weren't that great – they very much sound like they were written on the fly. I won't argue that *Horehound* sounds a little one-note compared to Jack's preceding albums, but it repays repeated listenings. It cultivates a very specific mood – late night, down-and-out, despondent yet defiant – that is pleasant to visit if not dwell in.

'60 Feet Tall' (Fertita, Mosshart)

This is a bold choice for the opening song, in that it's the second-longest song on the album and it's a very slow build. It starts with a distant rumble, before Mosshart enters with a slight muffling effect on her voice, sounding like she is calling from over the listener's shoulder. The song burbles along nicely, with a cute guitar figure and a nice bluesy solo, but it never really breaks out of its initial groove.

Mosshart's lyrics are classic blues braggadocio, boasting of how she can stand up to the evil ways of her no-good boyfriend. He may be 'cruel and shameless' and 'cold and dangerous', but she is 60 feet tall – a full ten feet taller than the 50-foot woman who attacked Hollywood in 1958. It is interesting to hear a woman deliver the kind of over-the-top boasts more typical of Robert Plant or David Coverdale.

'Hang You From The Heavens' (Fertita, Mosshart)

This was an interesting choice for a lead single, as it does not include the album's strongest hook or melody. But it did establish the general tone of the album: squelching organ intercut with growling guitar. Mosshart is even more forthright than on the opening song, boasting how little she cares about her lover's feelings:

I never know why I push you
Trash you just to confuse you
I make a hole just to see how
See through clean I can cut you

She alternately promises to hang him from the heavens – perhaps a metaphor for putting his weakness on display for all to see? – or drag him to the devil – a much more traditional blues allusion.

At the band's first gig, test pressings were given to fans that included covers hand-painted by the band members. Later, there were glow-in-the-dark and 8" 'Texas-sized' variants!

'Cut Like A Buffalo' (White)

This is Jack's lone solo writing credit on the album, and he sings lead for the only time here. He makes random gulps and moans that sound almost like beatboxing. Jack had a reflexive dislike of hip-hop, as did many a classic rock fan, as it gradually became the lingua franca of modern pop culture, but this song presages how even he would eventually integrate hip-hop influences into his sound.

Lyrically, the song is a series of laboured puns that allude to gender confusion and sexual indomitability. As to what 'cut like a buffalo' means? Buffalo are huge, powerful, untamed beasts, so one obvious interpretation springs to mind ... Then there is the line 'Cut a record on my throat, but the record's not broken'. I interpret this as Jack refusing to let people use his music against him.

This was the third single from this album and Jack directed the video. Actually, he directed two, because the first was not allowed in the UK. That version features Jack singing while women in veils (including his future wife Olivia Jean) menace him with knives. The second version features Jack miming like a silent film character while one woman belly dances.

'So Far From Your Weapon' (Mosshart)

This song is a slowly marinating stew of rumbling bass, swirling organ, ringing cymbals and subtle piano notes to add a bit of mystery. Like '60 Feet Tall', it seems like it will explode but never does. However, the vibe is just right for Mosshart's oblique outlaw story about a woman debating with her partner whether to stand and fight or hit the road.

'Treat Me Like Your Mother' (Fertita, Lawrence, Mosshart, White)

Now the album finally explodes, with a rude organ riff and a surging rhythm section. This song begins at maximum intensity and never lets up. It's yet another song about sexual power and mind games, but now it's as if Mosshart is furious that her previous warnings were ignored. She lays down the law in no uncertain terms, demanding respect from her man – albeit, of course, in the most oedipal manner possible:

Stand up like a man
You better learn to shake hands
And treat me like your mother

Jack sings the bridge and his entrance is suitably dramatic. It's unclear whether he is in dialogue with Mosshart, answering her charges, or if he's backing her up. His lines call out the kind of men who pretend to be good to get their own way – 'Mama's boys', you might say. The song climaxes with a chant – 'M-A-N-I-P-U-Late!' – that leaves no doubt about the band's opinion of these self-proclaimed 'nice guys'.

This was the second single from the album. The video by Jonathon Glazer, director of ace movies such as *Beast* and *Under The Skin*, consists of Jack and Mosshart firing machine guns at each other like it's a 21st-century cowboy duel.

'Rocking Horse' (Mosshart, White)

This is the slightest song on the album so far, and yet another drawing on outlaw imagery, with the odd religious reference for good measure. In classic antihero style, the narrator has given up on themselves and is trying to push their loved one away. Some Spaghetti Western twang takes this into Raconteurs' territory. Mosshart and Jack trade vocals, before singing together for the unnerving wordless climax.

73

'New Pony' (Bob Dylan)

The Western allusions continue with the second horse-themed song in a row. This one is a Bob Dylan cover, so, of course, the pony should be considered a metaphor for something. Dylan scholars, such as Clinton Heylin and Tony Attwood, interpret this song as Dylan aping Charley Patton's 'Pony Blues', and that the 'new pony' represents the blues itself, which Dylan adopted when he shifted from acoustic folk to electric rock in the 1960s. A song about a white man finding his identity through discovering old blues records? I can't imagine what Jack found appealing in that interpretation ...

The Dead Weather dispense with any ambiguity by stripping the lyrics down to the first few verses, and focusing on the one thing that riding a horse usually symbolises: sex. 'Come over here pony, I wanna climb up one time on you'. In theory, this was an ideal Dylan song for the band to cover: an album track from one of his less-acclaimed albums – 1978's *Street Legal*. But their stop-start arrangement and repetitive backing vocals leave this feeling like a slighter song than it originally was. Fertita's guitar solo is excellent, nonetheless.

'Bone House' (Fertita, Lawrence, Mosshart, White)

This song includes a first for Jack: a drum machine. This quickly gives way to 'real' drums and a honking organ. It is engaging at first, but excitement dissipates as there's no melody or hook to speak of. Mosshart, once again, asserts dominance over her target, this time, coming on like an obsessive girl in a Tim Burton movie: 'I build a house for your bones', 'I make a nest for your hair' and so on.

'3 Birds' (Fertita, Lawrence, Mosshart, White)

This is an instrumental, only Jack's second. It features a clipped funk riff with psychedelic guitar whoops and watery-sounding keyboards, but without a strong central motif, this feels like a backing track that nobody could be bothered to set words to.

'No Hassle Night' (Mosshart, White)

The title suggests that this is about a one-night stand, but it sounds more as if Mosshart is looking for a place to lay down and die. Once again, the song does not fully live up to its potential and seems to end just as it's warming up. The middle eight, where the surging keyboards are set against twinkling piano, is the best part.

'Will There Be Enough Water?' (Fertita, Mosshart)

The finale is the longest track on the album and the one that best exemplifies its slow, swampy aesthetic. It is more soundscape than song, with space for the instruments to breathe. Jack's acoustic guitar in between verses is especially great. The song this resembles the most, in its abstract evocation of the ocean, is The Beach Boys' 'Cool, Cool Water'. But, whereas that song saw Brian Wilson in childlike awe of this elemental force, this song sees Mosshart drawing on classic sailor song motifs:

> Will there be water when my ship comes in?
> And when I set sail will there be enough wind?

Jack sings the third verse, which includes the song's most revealing line: 'Just because you caught me, does it make it a sin?'. Maybe the title has a double meaning, referring to baptism? As in, will there be enough water to wash away all of Jack's sins? Not if that sin is making an underwhelming album. It would take The Dead Weather another go to win over disappointed critics.

Sea Of Cowards (2010)

Personnel:
Dean Fertita: guitar, organ, piano, synthesiser
Jack Lawrence: bass, drums
Alison Mosshart: vocals, guitar, maracas, synthesiser
Jack White: drums, vocals, guitar
Producer: Jack White
Recorded at Third Man Studio, Nashville, Tennessee, December 2009
Release date: 11 May 2010
Chart places: US: 5, UK: 32, Aus: 28

After their first tour, The Dead Weather went straight back into the studio to record this album, then went back on tour again, playing a further 48 gigs between March and July 2010. The album was released in the middle of the tour, less than a year after *Horehound*. As you might expect, the album is of a piece with their debut, albeit maybe a little tighter and sharper. These songs also feel less like they were formed out of jam sessions, and more like they were sculpted to play to the band's strengths – namely, Mosshart's strutting, sexually-charged energy and Jack's genre-warping eccentricity. This music sounds the closest Jack has come, thus far, to the gothic punk blues of his beloved Gun Club.

It feels like Jack's input was more to the fore on this album. For one, the title is Jack's slang for anonymous online critics, who, in 2009, were already saying that Jack had 'lost it' and were calling for him to reunite with Meg. Titling your album after an insulting term for your critics is all but guaranteed to ensure a frosty reception. However, this album was actually more warmly received than the debut by critics and fans alike. This was not only because Jack's songwriting voice was more evident, it was also that by releasing this album so soon after the last, The Dead Weather had proved themselves a real band and not a frivolous side-project. That meant people took more time to absorb and appreciate the music – and this is an album that reveals its pleasures with repeated listening.

Once again, I disagree with the general consensus and prefer the first album to its sequel. For all its faults, *Horehound*'s low and slow sound is substantially different from the rest of Jack's catalogue, whereas I find that this album's relentless antagonistic energy is comparable to *Icky Thump* and *Consolers Of The Lonely*, and it comes up short by comparison. That said, I do think this album includes some of the most entertaining *moments* in Jack's discography.

The album cover is also one of Jack's best, with the band dressed as participants in some kind of arcane ritual. Jack the Anglophile must surely have seen the 1974 folk horror classic *The Wicker Man*, and if he hasn't, he needs to get on that.

'Blue Blood Blues' (Fertita, Lawrence, White)
The album kicks off with a groovy riff that is gradually warped and twisted by sci-fi effects until it sounds like the song is being sucked into a black hole. Mossart is hard to hear on this, unless that's her speaking the distorted robotic backing vocals. She was probably wise to sit this one out, as it features Jack doing his goofiest 'badass loverboy' schtick. Get a load of these lyrics:

> And all the neighbours get pissed when I come home
> Lick an ice cream cone. Crack a bone
> Check your lips at the door woman
> Shake your hips like battleships

And best of all, Jack, the former alter boy, lets us know:

> Yeah, all the white girls trip when I sing at Sunday service

This song was the second single from the album, and the 12" vinyl contained a bonus 7" single inside – you had to saw it apart to get to it!

'Hustle And Cuss' (Lawrence, Mosshart)
Mosshart takes over and swaggers her way through one of the best songs on the album. It is little more than a funky groove, but it's a groove so funky it could have graced The Stones' *Exile On Main Street* – or even one of the Dr. John albums they drew from. It's also a demonstration of how vital shakers can be to a recording.
The opening couplet is among Mosshart's best lyrics, suggesting a world of mystery and frustration:

> Knock on the door and the door knocks back
> The joke never go no further than that

The rest of the song indicates a Jack White-esque sense of regret for childhood innocence lost, coupled with Mosshart's more overt sexual allusions:

> When we were young
> A different kind of fun
> Playing in the mud
> It meant something else
> Now we hustle and cuss

'The Difference Between Us' (Mosshart, White)
This starts off sounding like a classic Gary Numan song, with a cyclical machine-manipulated keyboard riff. It does not stay synthy for long, as ratt-a-tatt drums and processed guitars take over for another neurotic song. In this

case, Mosshart feels like she's losing her identity to her partner. 'I ain't doing so well', she cries, before the song segues into...

'I'm Mad' (Fertita, Lawrence, Mosshart, White)
...this bizarre track, which consists of Mosshart repeating the title phrase over and over. She whoops and hollers with abandon, but it feels a little like pantomime. Halfway through, there's a squealing feedback noise, like an old dial-up modem, and a Richie Blackmore-esque riff enters – and goes nowhere. As nice as it was to have a new Dead Weather album so soon after the first, tracks like these suggest that they should have taken more time.

'Die By The Drop' (Fertita, Lawrence, Mosshart)
This was the first single from *Sea Of Cowards*, and it feels like the first full-fledged 'song' on the album. There's even a proper chorus! The bare-bones riff is reminiscent of 'The Hardest Button To Button', and this song has a similarly intense build-and-release structure. This is another track about a toxic relationship. Despite Mosshart using the word 'brother', it is apparently about a married couple who are slowly destroying each other. To 'die by the drop' must be like the 'death by a thousand cuts' – it's the accumulation of all the little slights that really gets you. The song concludes with her digging a grave for them both. And you thought 'Death Letter' was grim!

This was the first single from the album. It reached number 20 on the Alternative Airplay chart and was the best-performing Dead Weather single of all globally.

'I Can't Hear You' (Fertita, Lawrence, Mosshart, White)
With that drama over, we return to the relatively subtler swamp blues of the first album. There are some tasty guitar licks, but little else of note musically. Mosshart sounds like she's singing from under the floorboards, and she gives a particularly campy performance as if she's waiting to jump out and scare us.

'Gasoline' (Fertita, Lawrence, Mosshart, White)
This song opens with 1960s-sounding fanfare, and it's driven by a curt organ riff that sounds like it was lifted from a horror film score. The squealing guitar duel is one of the highlights of the album. Mosshart sounds a lot like Jack here, although her lyrics are more blunt than even Jack's can be – she doesn't want a lovey-dovey man; she wants a machine.

'No Horse' (Fertita, Lawrence, Mosshart, White)
Another equine-themed song? Perhaps. There's no Western outlaw imagery here, only seething despair and self-hatred – which suggests that, in this case, 'horse' is slang for heroin. Mosshart paints a harrowing picture of someone stewing in their own isolation, doing what they can to keep their cravings at bay. This song is ugly and repetitive, but then so is heroin addiction.

'Looking At The Invisible Man' (Fertita, White)

This collaboration between Jack and Fertita brings out their most extreme qualities. Fertita's grinding electronically processed keyboards sound closer to Nine Inch Nails-style industrial rock than it does to the blues. Jack's vocals are also processed into chipmunk chirping, as if he is being subsumed into the music. The lyrics see him once again railing against critics who act like they know him.

'Jawbreaker' (Fertita, Lawrence, Mosshart)

This taught and fraught song sees Mosshart calling out some unnamed enemy. Musically, it makes me wonder if one of the unspoken influences on The Dead Weather was Uriah Heep. Classic 1970s songs of theirs, like 'Gypsy' and 'Easy Livin'', combined pounding one-chord guitar riffs with thick distorted keyboards in a similar manner to this song. Or rather, this song sounds like a third-generation photocopy of Uriah Heep. Specifically, the main verse riff sounds like the one from 'Joker And The Thief' by mid-2000s Australian thud rock revivalists Wolfmother. Hey, if you're gonna steal, steal from the best forgotten.

'Old Mary' (White)

This is the closest thing on this album to a major work from Jack because it's so bizarre that he simply had to make some kind of statement! It opens with a spoken-word section, in which Jack re-writes the 'Hail Mary' prayer. This is reminiscent of the Pink Floyd song 'Sheep', on which Roger Waters reworked the Lord's Prayer using *Animal Farm* imagery. Jack's version reimagines the Holy Virgin as some kind of ancient, all-consuming industrial mother figure:

Old Mary full of grease
Your heart stops within you
Scary are the fruits of your tomb
And harsh are the terms of your sentence
Old Mary, sister of mine
Mother to the world, carry this burden
Now until the moment of your last breath

That final line is recited over and over till the end of the song, like a fatalistic mantra. The music, combining ominous piano, guitars that resemble a printer running out of ink and what sounds like a baby crying, seems designed to drive the listener towards a panic attack. What an ace way to end an album.

Blunderbuss (2012)

Personnel:

Jack White: vocals, guitar, piano, electric piano, bass, drums

With:

Ruby Amanfu: backing vocals

Carla Azar: drums, maracas, percussion, shaker

Emily Bowland: clarinet

Bryn Davies: bass

Karen Elson: backing vocals

Joey Glynn: bass

Adam Hoskins: guitar

Olivia Jean: drums, guitar

Daru Jones: drums, tambourine

Fats Kaplin: fiddle, mandolin, pedal steel

Patrick Keeler: drums

Ryan Koenig: backing vocals

Pokey LaFarge: mandolin, backing vocals

Jack Lawrence: bass

Laura Matula: backing vocals

Jake Orrall: guitar

Lillie Mae Rische: fiddle

Brooke Waggoner: electric piano, organ

Producer: Jack White

Recorded at Third Man, Nashville, Tennessee

Release date: 23 April 2012

Chart places: US: 1, UK: 1, Aus: 2

All tracks written by Jack White, except where noted

The White Stripes officially broke up on 2 February 2011 via an announcement to the press. It seemed like a solo career was the natural next step. But, as with many Jack White projects, his first solo album had a spontaneous genesis. He had the Third Man Studio booked for a session with hip-hop legend RZA from Wu-Tang Clan, and when he failed to show, Jack decided to use the band he had prepared to record three new songs. Then, he simply pressed on, and *Blunderbuss* was born. As if to signal his artistic rebirth, he chose a new three-colour scheme – black, white and blue – that he has since used for every solo album.

For his first time recording an album, Jack did not have a band or a musical partner to answer to. This meant that he could pick and choose musicians as he needed them. His tendency towards whimsical gestures manifested in mainly using female musicians. Lest anyone think this was a 'token' gesture, these were all experienced musicians with great music of their own under their belt. For one, Olivia Jean leads an all-female garage rock band, The Black Belles, who were one of the first bands signed to Third Man Records.

When he took the album on tour – the first under his own name – he took the single-gender conceit further. He used two different bands – the all-female Peacocks and the all-male Buzzards – and decided which band played which show on the day of the concert. The musicians were quite reasonably frustrated by this, and touring with two full bands cost Jack a pretty penny. But that is a price one must pay to maintain a reputation as an eccentric weirdo.

Jack's reputation suffered a few blows when he divorced Karen Elson. In June 2011, they threw a party to celebrate their separation, and it seemed like they were amicable. But during a custody dispute in court, some of Jack's emails to Elson leaked, revealing humiliating private details. The thing the music press latched on to was Jack's bizarre antipathy towards the blues-rock duo The Black Keys, who he saw as following him in all things. The whole business made Jack seem petty and self-aggrandising. It led many people to interpret *Blunderbuss* as a divorce album – like Meg's beloved *Blood On The Tracks*. Jack has denied this, pointing out that Elson sings backing vocals on some songs. And, as always with him, the lyrics are open to different interpretations.

Despite those bad vibes, *Blunderbuss* had the best overall reception for a Jack White project since the first Raconteurs album. It was close enough to Jack's established sound that longtime fans did not feel cheated, and it was different enough not to seem like a stale rehash of past glories. More to the point, it is simply a collection of good songs, well-played and well-produced. Other Jack White albums may have set trends and inspired imitators, but this album, more than any other, feels like a timeless classic rock album that would have felt at home in 1972 as much as 2012.

'Missing Pieces'

To the surprise of some, Jack kicks off his solo career with a gentle electric keyboard riff. But lest we worry he's gone soft, a big distorted riff launches us into the song proper. The instruments enter one at a time in a deliberate-sounding manner, but the music still feels loose and organic. Jack lets the music breathe so we can take it in. And while his singing is still impassioned, it is less fraught and more free-flowing. He gives us two solos – on the guitar and the Rhodes piano. The overall impression is of a performer overbrimming with confidence.

Which makes the lyrics all the more striking in their fatalistic humour. Jack spins a tall tale in impressionistic fragments about a one-night stand that turns sinister. It starts with his nose bleeding in the shower, and ends with him waking up with his hands and legs cut off! The rag on the pillow next to him suggests he was drugged, like the urban legend about organ harvesting. It's a literalisation of how it feels when someone breaks up with you:

And they'll stand above you and walk away, yeah
That's right, and take a part of you with them

'Sixteen Saltines'

This song starts off sounding like The White Stripes, with its loveably basic three-chord riff, but then Jack turns on that grinding guitar tone and it morphs into The Dead Weather. What it lacks in a memorable chorus, it makes up for in energy and fascinating lyrics. The song's title references a snack that Jack's daughter requested, and it has no bearing on the rest of the song, which depicts romantic obsession in various archetypal and metaphorical ways. Jack, the paperboy, goes to deliver and notices that her 'pink mailbox' has been well-used. Ah, yes, very subtle. 'Who's jealous of who?' he asks repeatedly, as he sits alone, imagining another boy touching her. Jack might not have wanted us to read *Blunderbuss* as a divorce album, but these are not the lyrics of a man whose break-up left him in a good headspace.

This was the second single from the album, and the 12" vinyl was clear and filled with blue liquid.

'Freedom At 21'

Musically, this is one of Jack's best solo songs. This a modern-day rock song built from pieces of the past that sounds nothing like anything else. The combination of upright bass and a scattered, almost tribal drum pattern makes the song sound as if it is continuously lurching forward unsteadily. Jack lays on a surf guitar riff so tight that it veritably 'pops' out of the speakers. This is in contrast to the guitar solo, which sounds like DJ scratching. He also delivers one of his best vocal performances, wandering all over his range in a single verse.

What about the lyrics, though? Well, this is another portrait of an abusive woman:

Cut off the bottoms of my feet, made me walk on salt
Take me down to the police, charge me with assault
Smile on her face, she does what she wants to me

Is this a song about what Jack will put up with for the sake of a relationship? Unfortunately, no, it's about her lax morals in these modern times:

She don't care what kind of wounds she's inflicted on me
She don't care what colour bruises that she's leavin' on me
'Cause she's got freedom in the 21st century

Men feeling hard-done-by because women have too much freedom nowadays is not a good look. Especially if people assume you're talking about your ex-wife. But there is another layer to these lyrics:

Two black gadgets in her hands, all she thinks about
No responsibility, no guilt or morals cloud her judgement

So it's clear that the target of Jack's ire is not any one woman, or modern womanhood in general. Rather, he is despairing over the current generation's addiction to their mobile devices, broadcasting their private lives online and trash-talking other people with no thought of the consequences. Furthermore, 'She don't care what kind of things people used to do' – all this new-fangled technology is distancing people from their cultural roots. So Jack isn't a misogynist, just a regular grumpy old man! Jack's technophobia earned him some not undeserved mockery. This reached its peak around 2018 when he began requiring concert attendees to lock their mobile phones in special bags while the show was on.

This was the third single from the album, on 7" and digital, and there were also 1000 flexi discs that they tied to helium balloons as an advertising stunt. The video for this song muddies the thematic waters a little. It was directed by hip-hop trendsetter Hype Williams, and it tries a little too hard to make Jack seem like a leather-jacketed, sunglasses-wearing badass. As he's accosted by a scantily clad woman, it skirts too close to a lingerie ad.

'Love Interruption'
The album eases back for a few mellow tracks in a row. This is *Blunderbuss'* most enduring song, with an indelible melody and an earworm of a chorus. The music is simple but beautifully layered: acoustic guitar shadowed by electric piano, with a clarinet for texture and gorgeous backing vocals. The song never kicks into a higher gear, because it does not need to. Its straightforwardness is as warm and inviting as a vintage Christine McVie song. Even the lyrics feel timeless, drawing on the classic theme of the thin line between love and hate (also very Fleetwood Mac). Even if love can make him feel like he's been stabbed in the gut, and make enemies out of his friends, he still wants it. But now, he wants it on his terms: 'I won't let love disrupt, corrupt or interrupt me anymore'.

'Blunderbuss'
This is a lovely acoustic piano ballad, complete with strings and weeping pedal steel guitar (by the awesomely named Fats Kaplin). Nothing is overstated, not even the big final flourish, which cuts off just before it gets schmaltzy. This song might be based on Jack's real life, as one line about an exit 'Designed by men so ladies would have to lean back in their gait' could be referring to Karen Elson's exceptional height. The message seems to be that, while affairs might be selfish, they could be what the two paramours need. But, like the titular old-timey shotgun, affairs tend to blow up in your face.

'Hypocritical Kiss'
This opens with a theatrical piano flourish that threatens to get mawkish, but then it settles into a nice acoustic groove. The baroque piano breaks feel like

they were lifted wholesale from a different song and overlaid atop this one, but it works. Lyrically, this is a bitter song where Jack relays both sides of an argument. He is sorry he lost his temper, but she refuses to acknowledge that she is angry. She, in turn, calls out his patronising attitude. The reference to a 'dead brother' might lead one to assume this song is about him and Meg, but I hope it isn't.

'Weep Themselves To Sleep'
A dramatic opening gives way to a strident beat, dominated by Brooke Waggoner's piano playing that comes on like Liszt's Hungarian Rhapsody. It's more than the song deserves, as it has the weakest melody of the album. Halfway through, Jack's sputtering guitar invades the song and he plays his most discordant guitar solo yet. That reflects the song's disjointed meaning. It is a tribute to 'men who fight the world', who 'won't be left behind by time or any rules that try to bind them'. According to Nick Hasted's book, this song was inspired by hip-hop superstars like Jay-Z and Kanye West, whom Jack envies because their status in pop culture allows them to do and say what they want. Given that Kanye is now infamous for his anti-semitism, porn addiction and pathetic social media posts about his ex-wife, perhaps sometimes it is good having rules that bind you.

'I'm Shakin'' (Rudy Toombs)
This is a cover of a song first recorded in 1960 by Little Willie John. It's a representative example of horned-up 1950s R&B, and Jack and his band play it like they're a 1960s British beat group who've just discovered it: loose, energetic and, somehow, naive sounding, despite the raunchy lyrics. Jack throws in a reference to Rita Hayworth. 'My heart starts doin' that Saint Rita dance', he says, a pun on the term 'Saint Vitus Dance', a neurological disease that causes shaking. This was the fourth and last single from this album.

'Trash Tongue Talker'
This song is a homage to New Orleans pianist James Booker. 'That was the only song on the record that was directly influenced by another songwriter', said Jack to *Uncut*. He continued:

> I wanted to have a vibe in that song like some of his have, where it doesn't matter so much about the chords, it's a head tilted to the side presentation of the words. That was a new thing for me, to try and absorb directly what someone else has done. Despite what anyone says, I've never done that...

This features some wild piano playing, but no memorable hook. Jack is in strident haranguing mode. It reads like he is poking fun at trailer trash types who dish it out but can't take it, but in a broader sense, he is mocking gossip-spreaders in general. This song sounds a little underproduced compared to the rest of the album, especially in how Jack's voice is mixed to sound harsher and more brittle.

'Hip (Eponymous) Poor Boy'

This is a bouncy folk-pop shanty, with the kind of timeless melody that will make you certain you've heard it before. The arrangement, with mandolin to the fore, reminds me of The Kinks' underrated early 70s albums *Muswell Hillbillies* and *Everybody's In Show-Biz* – Americana from a semi-ironic outsider's point-of-view.

When Jack thought of the melody, he wrote down placeholder lyrics that included the word 'hippopotamus', and eventually, that word morphed into the title phrase. But who is the 'poor boy'? The line, 'Let the stripes unfurl, getting rich singin' 'Poor boy, poor boy'', suggests that he's singing about himself: a white man who got rich selling the Black man's blues. But Jack said to *NME* that 'the stripes' refers to the American flag, rather than his old band. But then there is the line, 'I'll be using your name', which surely must refer to his ex-wife's surname. Only John Gillis III knows the truth...

'I Guess I Should Go To Sleep'

This song is about needing to quit a domestic argument that you know you just can't win, but it does not invoke that stressful feeling. It is sung in tandem with backing vocalists Ryan Koenig and Pokey LaFarge, and that, plus the funky upright bass and rolling piano, make this reminiscent of one of Van Morrison's early 1970s albums, while the coda, with Jack lulling the listener gently to sleep, is more McCartney-esque.

'On And On And On'

This song's lovely instrumental opening sounds similar to, believe it or not, Yes – specifically, those times when Steve Howe's guitar sounds like keyboards, such as on 'Soon' (from 'The Gates Of Delirium'). The song proper has a gentle rockabye rhythm, with piano, strings and pedal steel guitar creating a meditative mood. That is appropriate for the existential lyrics, in which Jack laments the very idea of free will:

> The stones in the sky never worry
> They don't have to hurry, they move in their own way
> But I have to choose what to do
> How to act, what to think, how to talk, what to say

Envying inanimate objects because they don't have to change? Had Jack been reading the *Tao Te Ching*?

'Take Me With You When You Go'

Blunderbuss' final song sums up the album as a whole. It begins as a jaunty singalong with a jazzy rhythm. There's a lovely violin solo, which gives way to a cute little keyboard section. Then a big chunky riff enters, and Jack starts rap-singing. The backing vocalists join in with a similar frantic intensity as the Ikettes do on Frank Zappa's 'Montana'. This song is less lyrically dense than the rest of the album. After a series of songs about fraught relationships, Jack muses on whether he is too selfish to deserve love: 'My hands could be robbing without any knowledge... helping yourself could be hurting or harming someone'. The song ends with this feeling left unresolved...

Lazaretto (2014)

Personnel:
Jack White: vocals, guitar, piano, maracas, shaker, percussion
With:
Ruby Amanfu: backing vocals, shaker, tambourine
Carla Azar: drums, timpani
Ben Blackwell: drums
Bryn Davies: bass
Dominic Davis: bass
Doc: guitar, organ
Joey Glynn: bass
Adam Hoskins: guitar
Olivia Jean: percussion, backing vocals
Daru Jones: drums
Fats Kaplin: fiddle, mandolin, pedal steel
Patrick Keeler: drums
Ikey Owens: organ, keyboards, synthesiser, piano, electric piano
Catherine Popper: bass
Lillie Mae Rische: fiddle, mandolin
Timbre: harp
Brooke Waggoner: piano, organ, clavinet, synthesiser
Cory Younts: harmonica, synthesiser, mandolin, piano, shaker, backing vocals
Producer: Jack White
Recorded at Third Man, Nashville, Tennessee, 2012-2014
Release date: 10 June 2014
Chart places: US: 1, UK: 4, Aus: 3
All tracks written by Jack White

Blunderbuss established Jack White as a credible solo artist with his own sound and style, separate from his past bands. Now, the question was whether he would continue to develop that style or plough the same furrow. *Lazaretto* proved that Jack still had plenty more tricks in his bag. The key to his creativity, this time, was rediscovering, in an attic, a collection of short stories, poems and plays that he wrote when he was 19 years old. He used these as the basis for the lyrics, so that he was, as he said to *Rolling Stone*, 'collaborating with myself from the past'. But even as he drew from the past, this was his most forward-thinking album yet. He even – horror of horrors! – used digital editing software like ProTools. He also put even more effort into packaging and marketing his music.

The fan club exclusive edition was pressed on blue-and-white vinyl and was packaged with a 40-page hardcover book, a fold-out poster, a photo and a 7" featuring demos of 'Alone In My Home' and 'Entitlement'. But even that was eclipsed by the 'Ultra' edition, which showcased an abundance of features, such as flat edges; a side A that plays from the inside out and contains a hand-etched hologram; a side B with a matte finish; a song that plays differently depending on where you place the needle; and two tracks hidden beneath the centre labels – one track plays at 78 RPM, and the other at 45 RPM, making this a three-speed record. The LP also swaps the order of 'Entitlement' and 'Black Bat Licorice'. To people who accused him of using gimmicks to sell his music, Jack said in *Mojo*: 'Should we have told The Ramones to take off their leather jackets or the Jimi Hendrix Experience to shave off their afros, because that's not about the music either?'

Most of the pre-release hype, and also even most of the post-release discussion, focused on these gimmicks. This is frustrating because this arguably was Jack's most impressive collection of songs since *Elephant*, and it deserves to be recognised as such. But by 2014, hip-hop and pop were the dominant forces in popular music. The attention and acclaim went to albums like Taylor Swift's *1989* and Lorde's *Pure Heroine*. Forget Jack; amazing rock albums that could have been smash hits a decade ago, such as Against Me!'s *Transgender Dysphoria Blues* and Rival Sons' *Great Western Valkyrie*, were relegated to cult status. Even the ongoing vinyl revival mainly benefitted classic artists and pop stars, as no rock album released in the 2010s was among the decade's top-selling vinyl records.

Not that Jack needed to care. By now, Third Man Records was a self-sustaining system, and Jack was answerable to no one but himself. Among his recent achievements was a deal with Document Records to re-release classics by blues legends, including Charlie Patton and Blind Willie McTell. One could consider this to be Jack paying back the debt he owed to his undersung icons. He still had an eye on the past, even as his art moved inexorably forward.

'Three Women'

This is a perfect opener, as it samples all of the sounds Jack will use over the course of the album. It unfolds from a simple two-note organ riff into a full-band performance, with an especially slick interplay between the drums and piano. It's only until it's almost over that you realise there's barely any guitar, only wisps of pedal steel. But then a big fat riff ushers in the climatic solo, with harmonica joining in for extra rootsy flavour.

The lyrics are a sardonic update of Blind Willie McTell's 'Three Women Blues'. Like McTell, Jack is infatuated with three women: a redhead, a blonde and a brunette. Unlike McTell, he will use a digital photograph to decide. In a *Rolling Stone* feature, Jack used this as a defence against a journalist who accused him of having a 'woman problem'. He said that it's obvious he is singing 'in character' because the 'real' Jack White would never approve of digital photography!

Incidentally, in a 2012 *Uncut* article, it was revealed that Jack has different dedicated acoustic guitars for each of his previous groups, adorned with portraits of actresses from the Golden Age of Hollywood: Rita Hayworth (redhead) for The White Stripes, Veronica Lake (blonde) for The Dead Weather and Claudette Colbert (brunette) for The Raconteurs!

'Lazaretto'

Over a tight funk riff, Jack lays down some of his most absurd lines in a pugnacious style that verges on rapping. The song is a meta-commentary on hip-hop braggadocio. He shakes the hand of God, who is referred to throughout as 'she', as 'She never helps me out with my scams for free'. Is this Jack being a feminist or simply blaming another woman for his problems? There is also a passage in Spanish because Jack felt he would not get away with singing the line, 'I work hard!' – as if he hasn't made his intense work ethic a huge part of his personal brand. The narrator sings about being quarantined on the Isle of Man in a leper colony (the 'lazaretto' of the title). As he told *NPR*'s Bob Boilen, he was inspired by the idea of being locked away: 'I wish that some other forces, some powers that be, would push me into this scenario for a month and lock me somewhere, instead of me doing it to myself all the time'.

Really, though, this song is just an excuse for him to rock out. 'This is how I'm gonna do it!' he cries, before delivering a terrific guitar solo, blending fluid melodic lines with staccato bursts. After that, the song slows down for a steady, stomping riff and a whooping synthesiser breakdown. Then, the main riff resumes for a gorgeous violin solo. This is unmistakably rock music, but rock that sounds undeniably unique.

A live version of 'Lazaretto' was released as a 7" for Record Store Day on 19 April 2014. It was recorded and pressed to vinyl in under four hours, and sold by Jack outside the Third Man shop. This gave him the record for the world's fastest-released record, and that explains the etching by the runout grooves: side A 'Guinness'; side B 'Can Kiss My...'. You can hear this single version, and see it being recorded, on the Third Man Records' YouTube channel: OfficialTMR.

'Temporary Ground'

This starts as a country lament with mournful violin, then turns into a sweet song with lovely pedal steel from Fats Kaplin, exquisite piano from Brooke Waggoner and another violin solo from Lillie Mae Rische. Rische also sings the chorus, and with the tremor in her voice, she sounds like Emmylou Harris – the gold standard for country duet partners.

Jack's lyrics are about the impermanence of all things and humankind's quest for meaning. Some passages are reminiscent of Zen koans, ala 'What's the sound of one hand clapping':

Moving without motion
Screaming without sound
Across an open ocean
Lying there on temporary ground

That title phrase refers to a giant lily pad, the kind that can hold 1000 pounds. For Jack, this represents some kind of transitory state: a home with no foundation, the ground forever shifting under your feet.

'Would You Fight For My Love?

Once again, Jack had to insist that he was not writing about his divorce. As he said to *Mojo*:

> A lot of people will say: 'Oh, Jack went through a horrible divorce, so this album must be about that'. But would I want to sell and exploit my private life and that of my children, just to sell records? From day one, I've gone as far from personal experience as possible. I'm going to have to sing a song hundreds of times. I don't want to relieve a horrible event it was based on over and over.

Doth he protest too much? It's hard not to read this dramatic ballad as a divorce song. Jack sings of a one-sided relationship where he puts in all the work, even as he is scared of being hurt. Whether this is autobiographical or not, this is a sentiment people can relate to. Plus, the music is good enough to forgive Jack's spleen-venting. The opening bass rumble, tribal drums, portentous piano and wordless female vocals cultivate a widescreen sense of drama.

It gradually builds to a proper anthem, with a huge bass riff and chilly keyboards, as the backing vocals grow to a funeral chorale and Jack's vocal becomes more despairing. There is no catharsis, just a lingering sense of desperation.

'High Ball Stepper'

The opening 'yelp' came about because the steel guitar player, Maggie Björklund, was messing around with a pedal that reverses audio. Lillie Mae Rische made a sound while tuning up, and it created that screech. Jack had Ruby Amanfu double the sound with vocals, and that became the basis for this song. He used ProTools to edit part of the song and then printed it to tape to edit it further. Just like Jack to create more work for himself! The resulting instrumental sounds like 'Aluminum' all glammed up. Waggoner's piano playing resembles Mike Garson's for David Bowie – short melodic fragments and dramatic stabs. The music builds until the guitar lets out a rude burp that sounds like your speakers are torn. A series of short solos follow, and then just when you think it's over, there's a burst of noise – no doubt to remind vinyl listeners to turn the LP over.

This was the first music released as a teaser for the album; an odd choice, except that it ably demonstrates Jack's skills as a player and producer, separate from his songwriting. The single was a 7" vinyl with an etching on the B-side.

'Just One Drink'

Two versions of the same song on the same track? Anything is possible through the magic of vinyl! This song opens side two, and depending on where the player sets the needle down on the 'Ultra' edition of the LP, you get a different version of this song: a semi-acoustic version or an all-electric version. They play in separate grooves that sync up at 30 seconds. The electric version is the one included on all CD, download and streaming versions of the album, but I prefer the semi-acoustic version, if only for variety's sake. Both versions are indebted to 'Waiting For My Man' by The Velvet Underground, with its relentless stomping beat, but the use of violin and piano on this song gives it more of a rave-up flavour more suited to a drinking song than a heroin song.

Again, the theme is a dysfunctional relationship, but that comes second to references to classic blues tunes like Howlin' Wolf's 'I Asked For Water (She Gave Me Gasoline)' and Jack Dupree's 'Drinkin' Wine Spo-dee-o-dee'. There is a third version, all-acoustic, included on the *Acoustic Recordings* compilation.

'Alone In My Home'

Once again, piano is the star instrument, but here, Isaiah Owens' playing is similar to the spritely, playful style of Elvis Costello's Attractions sideman Steve Nieve. The melody is strong, and perhaps more suited to an extroverted anthem. Instead, this is Jack at his most Charles Foster Kane-like, reflecting the mood of the album's cover, which casts Jack as a lonely lord in a gothic garden under the gaze of stone angels, surveying his private fiefdom. He sings about isolating himself from potential enemies, and also friends, to protect himself from hurt: 'I'm becoming a ghost so nobody can know me'. Is Jack playing a character? Or is he being self-aware about his 'old before his time' persona?

'That Black Bat Licorice'

After a fractured vocal introduction comes a recurring spoken phrase – 'Behave yourself' – that resembles an early-2000s electro-pop hook from Swedish super-producer Max Martin. This song is little more than a syncopated keyboard and strings riff for Jack to rap over. Jack's lyrics are among his most absurdly funny. He boasts about his woman using words like 'avuncular', 'hypocaust' and 'Castrum Doloris'. He refers to Nietzsche and Freud, TV detective Columbo and Evangelical comics propagandist Jack Chick.

As to what the title means, your guess is as good as mine. It's something he needs to spit out, like these lyrics. The perfect melding of hip-hop swagger and rock flair comes when Jack cries, 'Make my fingers histrionic like this!', and launches into a blazing guitar solo. This song might be silly, but it's too ridiculously overconfident to dismiss.

'Entitlement'

Speaking of bitter old men, this song seems to reflect a reactionary mindset – at least on the surface. 'Entitled' is a charge that each generation levels against the next. But Jack may be on the side of the youth with these lines:

> There are children today who are lied to
> Told the world is rightfully theirs

The children are not the problem; it's that the world they will inherit 'may be spoiled' and is 'getting worse every day'. As Jack has it, selfish people ruin everything:

> 'Stop what you're doin' and get back in line'
> I hear this from people all the time
> 'If we can't be happy then you can't be too'
> I'm tired of being told what to do

Who are these people telling him what to do? Is it the entitled youth on social media? Or is he talking about critics, or ex-friends, or politicians trying to restrict people's rights? The slow country music is downbeat enough to make you feel like everyone is against you.

'I Think I Found The Culprit'

This is the least memorable song on the album, but it is still a solid tune, with a curt acoustic guitar riff and dramatic piano chords. The lyrics hint at romantic infidelity, with deeper underlying issues. Consider the chorus:

> Birds of a feather may lay together
> But the uglier one is always under the gun

Karen Elson was a supermodel, after all. Is Jack laying bare his insecurity regarding their relative attractiveness?

'Want And Able'

This song opens with crows cawing, taken from an old 1950s record used while hunting to attract the birds. It sets an appropriately ominous tone for a story that really seems to be about Jack's divorce. The line, 'Who is the who, telling who what to do?', is very, well, telling. Why did Jack change the characters at the centre of this fable from the biblical Cain and Able to Want and Able? It may be a pun, about the difference between what one partner wants, and what the other is able to give. This is a stately, well-constructed ballad, with every instrument nicely balanced, and nothing ostentatious to detract from the words. It ends abruptly, making for a less memorable finish than this album deserves.

Dodge And Burn (2015)

Personnel:
Dean Fertita: guitar, organ, piano, synthesiser
Jack Lawrence: bass, backing vocals, drums, guitar
Alison Mosshart: vocals, guitar, percussion
Jack White: drums, vocals, acoustic guitar
With:
Joshua V. Smith: cowbell
Cara Fox: cello
Elizabeth Lamb: viola
Kristin Weber: violin
Katelyn Westergard: violin
Producer: Jack White
Recorded at Third Man Studio, Nashville, Tennessee, 2013-2015
Release date: 25 September 2015
Chart places: US: 10, UK: 21, Aus: 21

The third Dead Weather album arrived without much fanfare, and, in truth, it came across as something like an afterthought. It was recorded in three weeks, spread over the three years 2013-2015, and was predominantly pieced together from snippets left over from the past two albums. Alison Mosshart wrote all the lyrics this time because Jack was extremely busy. Aside from his own music and his label, he also launched Third Man Books, which published underground poetry, and a culture magazine called *Maggot Brain*. If that wasn't enough, he also played a role in the launch of the streaming service Tidal. Tidal was designed to give a bigger cut of the revenue to artists and provide better sound quality for listeners – both things that appealed to Jack.

All these business dealings left Jack little to devote to promoting *Dodge And Burn*. A live performance on *The Late Show With Stephen Colbert* was his only promotion for the album. As a result, sales were modest, and reviewers glossed over it in anticipation of Jack's next solo effort. This is a shame because, in my opinion, it is a substantial improvement on *Sea Of Cowards* and features some of Mosshart's best songwriting. However, it seems, in retrospect, that this album is destined to remain a footnote for all but the most ardent Jack fans.

'I Feel Love (Every Million Miles)' (Fertita, Mosshart)

The first song already sounds more fully formed than *Sea Of Cowards*; less murky, less self-consciously histrionic, and what it lacks in eccentricity, it makes up for in immediacy. This is just a good old-fashioned shit-kickin' rock song, driven by a very Jack-like guitar riff from Fertita. Mosshart paints the impressionistic image of a post-apocalyptic landscape, pitching the band's Western fixations into sci-fi territory. This was the only charting single from this album, reaching number 27 on the US Alternative Airplay chart.

'Buzzkill(er)' (Fertita, Mosshart)

Now, we return to traditional Dead Weather territory. Fertita hops back on his keyboards – a Moog synthesiser that sounds like a dentist drill. Jack's drumming is especially impressive during the stop-start second verse, with its out-of-nowhere drum rolls. Nevertheless, despite each individual part of the song working, the whole never really catches fire. The lyrics seem like a continuation of the first song: Mosshart wandering alone, forsaken by God, like The Woman With No Name.

'Let Me Through' (Lawrence, Mosshart, White)

Mosshart does her usual vamp, putting herself in the mind of a bragging bully. However, disconcertingly, puny-sounding drums and a leaden one-note rhythm give this song a demo-like quality. Even the mid-song breakdown feels half-hearted, cutting off before it gets going.

'Three Dollar Hat' (Fertita, Lawrence, Mosshart, White)

This opens with a guitar figure reminiscent of, of all things, Metallica's nihilistic thrash ballad 'One'. Then, a discordant keyboard starts up as Jack takes his first lead vocal on the album, and he gets to rapping again. Then, the drums start rolling and the song goes into overdrive, with Mosshart singing, before Jack returns for the slow coda. This song is essentially a rewrite of the folk standard 'Stagger Lee'.

'Stag' Lee Shelton was an African-American pimp who, on Christmas 1895, murdered Billy Lyons in a saloon in St. Louis, after Lyons took Lee's hat. In one of folk music's more bizarre developments, a song written about the incident became a rock 'n' roll staple. Lloyd Price had a number-one pop hit in 1958 with an R&B take on the song, and it has since been covered by dozens of artists, including James Brown, Grateful Dead, The Clash and, of course, Bob Dylan.

The Dead Weather's rewrite amps up the lurid melodrama of the song, as the victim emphasises that he has a wife and kids. They changed Stag's name to Jackie and his victim's name to Johnny for no apparent reason, except maybe so Jack could insert himself into the story. The final lines add the twist that Jackie and Johnny love each other. But that still leaves this languishing in the shadow of Nick Cave & The Bad Seeds' blood-curdling version, which adds an explicit homosexual edge to the story. More to the point, Cave's version is a blistering assault on decorum and decency that leaves The Dead Weather's version in the dust.

'Lose The Right' (Fertita, Lawrence, Mosshart, White)

This is a more classic-sounding Death Weather song. The drums are rickety sounding, but this time in a cool, Tom Waits-ish way. It also has a doomy but upward-reaching guitar riff reminiscent of Black Sabbath, although, without Tony Iommi's power, it feels a bit forced. The guitar solo is pretty ordinary, too. But at least the lyrics are interesting, with Mosshart calling out people whose fear of hell makes them feel they have the right to judge others.

'Rough Detective' (Fertita, Mosshart, White)
This tune is built around a cute little riff, almost like a musical wolf whistle. Jack and Mosshart trade lines before joining in the chorus together. The lyrics are a jumble of noir fiction signifiers, and it's unclear if they are singing from the perspective of the suspect, the detective or the femme fatale. By the end, they've descended into maniacal laughter. For the last 20 seconds, it slips into another riff that sounds like it could be going somewhere interesting but just stops.

'Open Up' (Mosshart, White)
After a dramatic opening, followed by a soft section, a huge slashing guitar riff enters and it becomes a fairly straightforward garage rocker. But it has one of the album's strongest melodies, and Mosshart delivers it with a real sense of desperation. Her lyrics are difficult to decipher, but the predominant motif seems to be the struggle to communicate:

My hand is faster than the pen but the end has been written down
Still the ink will not dry, undermined by a hope that I'm wrong

It is as if she is torn between the need to express herself and a fear of vulnerability. The chorus expresses ambivalence: 'Open up, open up... That's enough, that's enough'.

'Be Still' (Fertita, Lawrence, Mosshart, White)
This opens with a lo-fi percussion track mixed to sound as if it was sampled. This is, perhaps, another lift from Tom Waits; compare it to 'Eyeball Kid' or his cover of 'Heigh Ho'. It quickly gives way to more swaggering bluster and lyrics that are little more than crime fiction word association. Mosshart sings lead and Jack joins in on the chorus. The highlight is a cool guitar versus keyboard riff-off at the very end.

'Mile Markers' (Fertita, Lawrence, Mosshart, White)
This is one of the best songs on the album, if only because it breaks the format. This is like techno music played by a band instead of a machine. It includes some of Jack's most dexterous drumming, a clattering cacophony that resembles the barrage of 1990s drum-n-bass, while the chorus feels like it was lifted from Donna Summer's album *Bad Girls*. The Dead Weather go disco? It could have been a disaster, but Mosshart sells the song with her cocky delivery, like patter in a classic screwball comedy. This includes one of her best lines: 'Big boys, bad girls, grind their teeth in stereo'. The steady building urgency of the song helps us feel for Mosshart's protagonist, a

woman on the road trying to outrun her dodgy past ('I lost track of all the money') and fixating on strange details ('Now I just count mile markers'). It's also implied that her lover is a prisoner or a soldier, and perhaps that those are equivalent:

When you finish out your sentence
Dear soulmate, behind stripes and stars

'Cop And Go' (Fertita, Mosshart, White)
A one-note keyboard pulse runs through this entire song, with stinging guitar riffs over it. It feels like the band are really cooking now, even if it took almost the entire album to get there. This song feels like an extension of the preceding tracks: Mosshart playing the haunted paranoid loner. She gets especially heated in the lead-up to the finish, and it's a shame the lyrics don't amount to more than an abstract picture.

'Too Bad' (Fertita, Mosshart)
This is another song that does not add up to much, but the band's performance is so in the pocket, that it is pointless to complain. Lyrically, this reads as if Mosshart's occasional allusions to being a 'woman on the lam' have come full circle. It's like a film noir, where the protagonist is being interrogated by the police and they start narrating the tale in flashback:

I know where the body is
I know why the branches twist
And when the well is getting low
How it came to be so

I know how the story ends
I know who dies, I know who lives

'Impossible Winner' (Mosshart)
This is Mosshart's masterpiece. If the preceding song wrapped up the album's impressionistic crime story, this is the denouement where we learn what was driving the protagonist all along. Again, Mosshart draws on cliched Western and crime fiction tropes, but now there's a clearer indication of what these things represent. In the other songs, she merely wanders through the landscape; now, she says, 'I am the desert sun' and 'I am the wilderness'. This whole album has been a journey through her own subconscious:

I am a wheel going round
In a mirror house
A maze with no way out
What you have fears about

She fights those fears and emerges broken but resolute, finding herself at last:

Drag my body through the sand
Drag my body down the road
Drag me off to the end
Turn around, here I am

Against all odds, she has survived; she is 'The Impossible Winner'. But it's a pyrrhic victory when it involves putting her weaknesses on display for others to see:

I'll be here every night
My name up in lights

Mosshart delivers these lyrics without any distortion or distancing effects on her voice, as if she is finally ready to show her 'real' self.

This would all be pop-psychology navel-gazing if the music wasn't equally as good. With a measured beat, big piano chords and a soul-stirring string arrangement (with an actual quartet, not a synthesiser), this is the closest Jack has come to playing on a big, lighter-waving, 1980s-style power ballad – and I don't mean that derisively.

The black-and-white music video is also impressive. Inspired by Todd Browning's *Freaks*, by way of *The Addams Family*, it features the band members with different physical deformities, playing while trapped in cages.

Boarding House Reach (2018)

Personnel:
Jack White: vocals, guitar, piano, maracas, shaker, percussion
Bobby Allende: percussion, drums
Carla Azar: drums
Anthony Brewster: synthesiser, organ
Justin Carpenter: trombone
Louis Cato: drums, guitar, bass
Dominic Davis: bass
Neal Evans: synthesiser, organ, piano
Joshua Gillis: guitar
DJ Harrison: synthesiser, keyboards
Daru Jones: drums
Fats Kaplin: fiddle
Neil Konouchi: tuba
Ann McCrary: backing vocals
Quincy McCrary: piano, synthesiser
Regina McCrary: backing vocals
Gianluca Braccio Montone: piano samples
Ian Montone: piano samples
Charlotte Kemp Muhl: bass
Neon Phoenix: bass
Justin Porée: percussion, udu
Esther Rose: backing vocals
Kevin Smith: trumpet
C. W. Stoneking: spoken word
Brooke Waggoner: piano
Producer: Jack White
Recorded at Third Man, Nashville, Tennessee; Sear Sound, New York City, New York; Capitol, Hollywood, Los Angeles, 2017
Release date: 23 March 2018
Chart places: US: 1, UK: 5, Aus: 8
All tracks written by Jack White, except where noted

By 2017, not only was Jack White on top of the world, but his success had trickled down. Third Man Records was thriving, as one of the cultural centres of the now-thriving Nashville alternative scene. But it was not just Jack's adopted home that benefitted; his old hometown Detroit reaped some of the spoils. In 2016, he opened a vinyl pressing plant in the Cass Corridor district, which became a crucial part of the supply chain for the physical media market he had long championed. Of course, once you've reached the top, the only way to go is down...

For his third solo album, Jack changed the way he wrote. As he told *The New Yorker*, he wanted to imagine a song into existence, the way Michael

Jackson did. He wanted to 'do everything in my head and to do it in silence'. So, based on these mental notes, he recorded the basic instrumental parts for this album by himself, with guest musicians adding textures and highlights after the songs were written.

The result was *Boarding House Reach*, the first album of Jack's to have a generally negative reception. Publishers that were usually on Jack's side, such as *The Guardian, Pitchfork, The A.V. Club* and *AllMusic,* gave it middling scores. Tom Breihan of *Stereogum* absolutely tore it apart: 'Even taking into account all his various bands and side projects, this is the worst album that has ever borne the man's name... It sounds like a man disappearing permanently up his own asshole'.

There are many albums by great artists that were greeted derisively upon release but have now been reclaimed as neglected classics. Sometimes, they were ahead of their time (for instance, Paul McCartney's self-titled debut is now considered a pioneer of the lo-fi genre) or they changed too much too fast (it now seems absurd how widely loathed Lou Reed's masterpiece *Berlin* was, due to it being measured against the far more fun *Transformer*). Neil Young practically built his career around defying audience expectations. Every artist should feel empowered to swim against the fickle tides of popular culture in order to stay true to their unique personal vision.

The problem with *Boarding House Reach* is that Jack's 'vision' is utterly befuddling. He made an album for an aesthetic that does not yet exist: cybernetic beat poet meets new-wave gospel. On paper, that sounds more interesting than it is. He mostly ditched the hard-hitting riffs and tight-but-loose band feel and added synthesisers, electronic beats and spoken word interludes. Let me be clear: the problem with *Boarding House Reach* is not that Jack tried new sounds and pushed himself creatively; it's that he did so at the expense of writing great songs. Breihan accurately asserted: 'Thirty seconds after listening to *Boarding House Reach*... you will not be able to hum one single moment of one single song'. This lack is compounded by the album's chaotic sequencing, where, just as it seems to be hitting a groove, it lurches in another direction.

All that said, when Jack toured the album with a full band, everyone agreed that these songs sounded much better live. Also, this album repays repeated listening, especially as, in this age of streaming, one can reorder the tracks to create a more cohesive listening experience. For what it's worth, here is my trimmed and re-shuffled track order: 'Corporation', 'Over And Over And Over', 'What's Done Is Done', 'Get In The Mind Shaft', 'Why Walk A Dog?', 'Connected By Love', 'Ice Station Zebra', 'Respect Commander', 'Hypermisophoniac', 'Humoresque'.

'Connected By Love'
The album opens disconcertingly, with an ominous throbbing synthesiser line. It has a pace and timbre similar to 'Requiem' by industrial rock innovators Killing Joke, but this synth sounds more 'plastic'. The drums

enter at a steady pace and they also sound synthetic. Jack's voice is the first 'real' thing we hear, and he is eventually joined by female backup singers, followed by a solo on what sounds like a church organ. Perhaps Jack was aiming to make a point by contrasting iconic signifiers of Black musical 'authenticity', from the gospel tradition, with this ostentatiously artificial backing music, but the point does not come across because the song is so trite. It works as a kind of retro-pop kitsch artefact, but the clichéd lyrics leave a hollow feeling. David Bowie used the term 'plastic soul' to describe his album *Young Americans*, but with that, he used the musical idiom to subvert iconic images of American youth culture. By contrast, 'Connected By Love' sounds like imitation soul music made by plastic people. As the album's first single, this was an ominous sign.

'Why Walk A Dog?'

This demonstrates my point about the album's terrible pacing. Jack follows a questionable opening track with this laboured song, which consists mainly of a dolorous drum machine rhythm, synthesiser bursts that resemble soap opera stings and a lethargic fuzz guitar solo. The whole song is a complaint, barely disguised as an extended simile. Jack asks and answers the title question: dogs need to be walked because, otherwise, they are stuck in a life of deadening domestic servitude. Aptly, it resembles how musicians can feel trapped by record contracts, with performing as their only outlet. It's all a bit petulant, and not helped at all by a reference to a much, much better song: the line, 'What is so funny about beasts above understanding?', brings to mind 'What's So Funny (About Peace, Love And Understanding)?' by Nick Lowe/Elvis Costello.

'Corporation'

If this album has a defining statement, it is this track. Despite being mostly instrumental, it shows where Jack's head was when making this album, as he sings:

Yeah, I'm thinking about starting a corporation.
Who's with me?
Nowadays, that's how you get adulation

Jack told *The Sun* that these lyrics were inspired by Donald Trump. However, they also serve as a criticism of the modern music industry, where the major stars are as much a 'brand' as an artist, with their music merely one 'service' they offer as part of a sprawling money-making enterprise.

Nevertheless, this song is not an angry screed; it's an ironic rave-up. Jack doesn't even start singing until three minutes in. The song is mostly a funk jam, and, in this case, the artificial-sounding production adds to the feel instead of detracting from it. It resembles classic Stevie Wonder or Prince: a futuristic take on funk. More importantly, it brings some much-needed energy to the album. Live, this became a great showcase for his band. There is also a swanky music video where the song is intercut with scenes of a detective investigating Jack's murder.

'Abulia And Akrasia'

We're three songs in and it still hasn't felt like the album has really begun. So, what better time to drop in a spoken word piece? And one not even spoken by Jack! Many people assumed that the speaker was actor Woody Harrelson, what with the broad Texas drawl and even broader acting. But the vocalist is C.W. Stoneking, an Australian bluesman. Jack liked the man's voice so much that he wrote this poem for him to recite. As he said to *Global News*: 'It was basically me trying to find as many words as I could that I wanted to hear him say because I love his speaking voice. How can I make the most complicated poem about wanting a cup of tea?'

And yes, that is indeed what the poem is about. With only acoustic guitar and trumpet for accompaniment, Stoneking recites Jack's ostentatiously loquacious verse with all the import of Macbeth's soliloquy. One interpretation of this track is that it's an affectionate parody of art rock pretentiousness. A less charitable interpretation is that it is indistinguishable from what it's parodying. Incidentally, 'Akrasia' refers to a lack of self-control, which is what Jack is demonstrating here, and 'Abulia' refers to a lack of motivation, which is what listeners feel when they consider replaying this track.

'Hypermisophoniac'

This is another half-formed sketch of a song, but this time, there's a reason for it. 'Misophonia' is a psychological phenomenon where certain aural stimuli provoke a reflexive negative response. A 'hypermisophoniac' would, therefore, be a person with an extreme aversion to specific sounds. When Jack discovered the concept, he was inspired to create something beautiful using annoying sounds. He succeeded with the second part, at least.

The song starts with the sound of his son's fidget cube, manipulated to sound like, as Jack said in an interview with Los Angeles' ALT 98.7 FM radio station, 'Pop Rocks going off in your mouth'. There's a recurring synth swoop throughout that sounds like a video game character receiving a power-up. Vocals weave in and out, some distorted to a chipmunk squeak. There's a guitar solo and a bass solo, but the piano is the only sign of organic life. If you fed a handful of mid-70s Todd Rundgren albums into ChatGPT and told it to write you a song, this could be the result.

'Ice Station Zebra'

And here is yet another song comprised of bits and pieces. There's an intense thrash riff, cabaret piano and an udu (a Nigerian jug instrument). The difference between this and the preceding song is that this is fun to listen to. One reason for that is Jack's rapping, in full-on, old-school Run-DMC 'rock the mic' mode for the first half, and then a less aggressive jazzy scat-singing style for the second half.

This song's title comes from the 1963 book by Alistair McLean, which was adapted into a film in 1968 by John Sturges. The story is not referenced directly in the lyrics, but Jack was likely inspired by the legend that the reclusive OCD-afflicted tycoon Howard Hughes watched this film hundreds of times. And we were worried when Jack looked to Charles Foster Kane as an inspiration...

The lyrics reference the 1967 prison film *Cool Hand Luke*, one of the definitive 'man against the system' stories. There are also nods to James Brown and the painter Caravaggio, both famously combustible artists. So is this rap a tribute to artistic individualism, or worse, Jack's own ego? No, the message is more inclusive, and incisive, than that. Jack talks to a hypothetical mentee about how artists are labelled as part of a genre or movement, usually against their will. But this won't limit them if they don't let it:

> Truth, you're the warden, here's the keys to the prison
> You create your own box, you don't have to listen
> To any of the label makers, printing your obituary

Ultimately, says Jack, every artist is beholden to those who came before, and it's pointless to pretend otherwise:

> If Joe Blow says 'Yo, you paint like Caravaggio'
> You'll respond 'No, that's an insult, Joe;
> I live in a vacuum, I ain't coppin' no one'
> Listen up, son

Unlike some other artists, who try to pretend they invented what's cool, Jack has never been shy about citing his influences – it's one of his most endearing qualities. But he also initially seemed hesitant to expand his range of influences. This song is Jack looking back at the young man who wrote 'Little Room' and telling him it's going to turn out okay. The key idea is that every artist is part of a rich creative legacy, a great chain linking back to the original creator:

> Everyone creating is a member of the family
> Passing down genes and ideas in harmony
> The players and the cynics might be thinking it's odd
> But if you rewind the tape, we're all copying God

'Over And Over And Over'

This is the only song on this album that wouldn't sound out of place on a Jack White garage rock mix tape, and that's because it dates back to 2005. A catchy riff and a strong chorus hook bring to mind past glories – at least until the demented synth solo, which is followed by a bongo breakdown. The gospel backing vocals add a touch of high drama, although, at points, they are also distorted into inhuman sounds. Interestingly, for what counts on this album as a throwback, this song was once intended for a project with rapper Jay-Z. When that fell through, Jack had trouble nailing the song, suggesting that retro-rock was not where his head was at.

As for the lyrics, Jack compares himself to Sisyphus, the king from Greek mythology who was cursed in the afterlife to roll a boulder uphill over and over for eternity. He also cites the line 'Who could not win the mistress, woo'd the maid' from Alexander Pope's 'An Essay On Criticism: Part 1'. That poem is about critics who turn on the artists they once supported. This reference suggests that Jack sees his battle against critical brickbats as a kind of Sisyphean struggle. However, when he attempts to rhyme the name of Italian car manufacturer Isotta Fraschini with the word 'perfidy', as he does here, he should be willing to accept some constructive criticism.

'Everything You've Ever Learned'
This opens with a repetitive voice-over, like the narrator of a 1950s educational film stuck on a loop. Then, over buzzing guitars and bongos, Jack recites a series of vague homilies, mixed to sound as if he was far away, perhaps preaching from atop a distant mountain. Then, the drums enter with big keyboards and Jack almost drowns himself out. Perhaps he represents the spirit of common sense being swamped by the information age. The final line is the best clue and one of the few real pieces of insight on the album:

Do you wanna question everything?
Then think of a good question

'Respect Commander'
After a false start, this song hits on an impossibly fast groove. The drums, by Jack and Bobby Allende, are so fast that Jack was worried they wouldn't be able to perform the song live. The lengthy instrumental introduction includes synthetic orchestral stabs ala Trevor Horn's productions for Yes and Art Of Noise. There is a brief vocal section where Jack sings about his desire for women to control him. That's followed by an ecstatic solo, his best guitar moment on the album.

'Ezmerelda Steals The Show'
This is a double-tracked spoken-word piece over gentle organ and folk guitar picking. Jack was inspired by the recitals at his children's school to write this fable about a girl calling out the audience with a performance art piece. Like most performance art, this song has the germ of an interesting idea but is made hard to bear by its pretentiousness.

'Get In The Mind Shaft'

Oh good, more spoken word! Does Jack worry that his music is getting in the way of his message? The gimmick this time is that there are ten different versions of this opening narration, available on different editions. The 'default' version – on the digital release – is about Jack discovering the power of piano chords. The other versions are about: Jack's memory of seeing ghosts; miners trapped underground; the universal dignity of hands-on labour; a crisis of identity with a fisherman; playing baseball in the hot sun; the interconnectedness of all natural things; existential dread brought on by a metaphorical cosmic hum; and the magic of music making. If that all sounds like a bit too much, the rest of the song does little to allay confusion. The remaining lyrics are distorted into a cyborg whine, and the music sounds like a combination of Angelo Badalamenti's *Twin Peaks* theme, Meco's disco-fied *Star Wars* novelty single and a SoundCloud rapper.

'What's Done Is Done'

Now we return to some genuine human feeling, with Jack's and Esther Rose's singing unadorned by effects. But the faux-gospel vibe is undermined by the stiff drum sound. Things liven up when the church organ enters and 'real' drums take over. Then there's a synth solo that resembles Bernie Worrell's playing on classic Parliament-Funkadelic records, which became familiar to others of Jack's generation via being sampled on G-funk songs by the likes of Dr. Dre and 2Pac. Perhaps fittingly, the lyrics have a gangsta rap vibe, being about two ex-lovers about to square off with firearms. That's the more upbeat interpretation; the other is that it's about suicide.

'Humoresque' (Antonin Dvořák, Howard Johnson)

This song has the craziest credits in pop music history. The music was adapted from an 1894 composition of the same name by Czech composer Antonín Dvořák. The lyrics are credited to Howard Johnson, but they were actually composed (or at least adapted) by infamous gangster Al Capone! He hand-wrote the lyrics while in prison, and Jack paid almost $19,000 for the sheet at auction in 2017. As far as absurd, indulgent, 'I have more money than is good for me' rockstar purchases go, this is more interesting than a private jet or a solid gold toilet.

What can we say about Capone's lyric writing? This is a straightforward love song, and it is surprisingly sappy for a man who ordered the murders of multiple people. Capone relies on the most basic and overused metaphors, e.g. music, flowers, gentle breezes. I would say that he was as good at lyric writing as he was at paying his taxes.

This is almost a lullaby, with melancholy piano chords rising and falling against jazzy drums, and Jack at his most gentle sounding. If this came at the end of any other album, it would feel like a genuinely sweet moment. Here, it seems like one final fake-out.

Help Us Stranger (2019)

Personnel:
Brendan Benson: vocals, guitar, percussion, harmonica
Patrick Keeler: drums, percussion, backing vocals
Jack Lawrence: bass guitar, guitar, synthesiser, backing vocals
Jack White: vocals, guitar, piano, synthesiser
With:
Dean Fertita: piano, synthesiser, guitar, organ
Lillie Mae Rische: violin
Scarlett Rische: mandolin
Joshua V. Smith: organ, backing vocals
Producer: The Raconteurs
Recorded at Third Man, Nashville, Tennessee, June 2018-January 2019
Release date: 21 June 2019
Chart places: US: 1, UK: 8, Aus: 23
All tracks written by Brendan Benson and Jack White, except where noted

The Raconteurs had been silent since six gigs in 2011, and in the interim, their reputation had grown somewhat, especially amongst second-generation fans. It is not uncommon to read comments under Jack White videos from people who discovered him via The Raconteurs rather than The White Stripes. So their return was greeted with grateful surprise ... and a little apprehension. After all, supergroups reconvening after a long time apart have typically delivered substandard products. See, for example, *American Dream* by Crosby, Stills, Nash & Young and *Union* by Yes. It can be hard to recapture a sense of collective camaraderie when an artist has spent years refining their individual artistic style. But remarkably, this was not a problem for The Raconteurs. This album sounds like it was recorded in 2011 and sealed in a vault until now.

It is a double-edged compliment to say that this album is on par with *Broken Boy Soldiers* and *Consolers Of The Lonely*. It's less aggressive and more rustic than the latter but not as inventive as the former. It is, to put it bluntly, a pleasant collection of solid songs performed with vigour by professional musicians – no more and no less. It neither disgraces The Raconteurs' good name nor provides a compelling reason for their continued existence. If this sounds like I am damning this album with faint praise, that is only because Jack and the band have set such high standards for themselves. It did serve the important function, following the mechanised *Boarding House Reach*, of assuring fans that Jack had not lost touch with his roots. Thus, it became The Raconteurs' first number-one album on the *Billboard* chart.

'Born And Razed'
This starts gently, with some guitar noodling reminiscent of an early 1970s jam band (it makes me think of the Welsh band Man). Very soon, though, a

big rock riff arrives and the song kicks straight into fourth gear. The band sound completely in lockstep and the message is clear: The boys are back in town! Jack sings the verses, about living fast in dens in inequity, while Benson undercuts such cliches with the chorus, singing about the women he pines for.

'Help Us Stranger'

This opens with Jack singing over an acoustic guitar, mixed to sound fragile and worn like an old country blues 45. The recurring line, 'Brother can you spare the time?', evokes the classic of the Depression-era standard, 'Brother, Can You Spare a Dime?', and this song has a similar theme of looking out for others in need. After the evocative introduction, the track skips and the song proper begins. It has an unusual arrangement, with a fat, aggressive bass sound, exotic Egyptian percussion and cymbals mixed unusually high so that it sounds like there is a toy train chugging through the song. Jack and Benson sing in unison, their voices blending better than ever before.

'Only Child'

Benson leads this sombre folk rock song about childhood innocence giving way to despondency. There are two short, spiky guitar solos, as well as a brief recurring sci-fi keyboard riff. This song is the heretofore undiscovered mid-point between Bob Dylan and The Alan Parsons Project.

'Don't Bother Me'

Jack leads this raucous electro-punk track, driven by the title phrase chanted as if by a malfunctioning robot. There's a cool guitar solo that sounds like it's using both the phase pedal and the vocoder at the same time, plus a short climactic drum solo from Keeler – the first of such on a Jack album!

Jack sings with real venom, making one wonder who the song's target is. The first verse sounds like a general gripe against social media ('All your clicking and swiping'). But the second verse seems to take indirect aim at alt-country singer-songwriter Ryan Adams, what with the phrases 'political science' and 'easy tiger' (referring to an Adams song and album, respectively). It is unknown what Adams did to earn Jack's enmity, but it is worth noting that, around the time this album was released, Adams faced a public reckoning over allegations of sexual impropriety throughout his career (hence the line, 'Your 'who me?' fake apologies'). It is possible that Jack's beef with Adams goes all the way back to 2003, as this song recalls 'Black Math' somewhat, with its similar breakdown section.

'Shine The Light On Me'

This song combines influences from three rock legends. The opening harmonies are reminiscent of The Beach Boys circa *SMiLE*; the phrasing of the hook, 'Ooh, what can you do, love?', is Beatle-esque; and the song as a whole – but especially the outro – has the rock gospel feel of The Rolling Stones' classic 'Shine A Light'. However, this song is unable to transcend its influences because the band don't push any of these elements far enough to achieve a rapturous release. Fittingly, it is a song about the struggle to find creative inspiration.

'Somedays (I Don't Feel Like Trying)'
This song is where all the rapture went. It begins with a catchy blues guitar riff and a swinging beat, and builds to an ecstatic mantra. Benson sings with real soul, as if he is battling against the doomy chorus riff. There is also a gospel organ buried in the mix, fighting to be heard. The lyrics tell of a struggle against depression and doubt, in such honest and earnest terms – no obfuscating metaphors this time – that the song has universal appeal. It culminates with the phrase, 'I'm here right now, I'm not dead yet', repeated over and over as the music ascends. Once again, Benson delivers an album highlight by playing things straight down the middle and hitting the target dead-on.

'Hey Gyp (Dig The Slowness)' (Donovan Leitch)
This is a cover of a song by Donovan, one of the most underappreciated 1960s artists. Donovan practically invented psychedelic folk – or, at least, the extremely British version of the genre that focused on fairy tales and faux-Eastern mysticism. It's easy to see how Donovan's child's-eye view of the world appealed to Jack, but this particular song is not in that mode. The lyrics are about offering to buy your love various things, a cliché as old as pop music. So, instead, the song is an excuse for the band to wail on their instruments. The highlights include astonishingly fast and nimble drumming from Keeler and a harmonica solo from Benson. While it would have been cool to hear The Raconteurs cover, say, 'Hurdy Gurdy Man', this is a fine example of Jack covering forgotten gems instead of obvious songs.

'Sunday Driver'
This is solid, reliable rock 'n' roll: a catchy riff and a rudimentary melody, embellished with sci-fi wah-wah guitar and dazed harmonies in the bridge. It is part of the grand tradition of 'automobile as metaphor' songs, which includes The Beatles' 'Drive My Car' and Bruce Springsteen's 'Pink Cadillac'. In this case, the 'Sunday driver' refers to some nogoodnik out to seduce the narrator's sister. This was originally released as a double A-side with the following song as part of the Third Man Records exclusive Vault Package for the *Consolers Of The Lonely* Ten-Year Anniversary Special Edition.

'Now That You're Gone'
An old-fashioned soul ballad from Benson – complete with a doo-wop chord sequence and extremely literal woe-is-me lyrics – is invaded by Jack's

dentist drill guitar needling. Mention should also be made of the throbbing, synthetic-sounding bass.

'Live A Lie'
This is a punkish, garage rock blast, basically an excuse for a neat pun: 'I just wanna lie with you'. 'Lie' as in sleep with and lie as in 'I just wanna live a lie with you'. Benson sings, but the sentiment that a relationship might work better when the partners hide the truth from each other is very Jack-like.

'What's Yours Is Mine'
Another fairly rudimentary song about a possessive relationship. This one has a tight, funky riff, but it stops just when it seems to get going.

'Thoughts And Prayers'
The Raconteurs once again save the best for last. While this is not an epic on the scale of 'Carolina Drama', it is the most ambitious track on this album. Some distant piano and delicate acoustic guitar picking set a sombre mood. There are Vangelis-like low synth notes throughout, and the contrast between these machine sounds with Scarlett Rische's mandolin and Lillie Mae Rische's fiddle is striking. The long drag on the strings going into the second verse primes the listener for the climactic fiddle solo, which lifts this song into the stratosphere.

This song seems easy to interpret on the surface, but it has layers. The title phrase has, in recent years, become a morbid joke. It refers to the kind of meaningless 'motherhood statements' that American politicians drop to the press after a tragedy – usually a mass shooting – in lieu of actually doing something productive. But the phrase does not appear in this song's lyrics, which are more insular. The first few verses see the narrator struggling against existential ennui, contemplating the friends and family they've lost. But maybe the personal is political? For they turn their focus to humanity at large with this key line: 'And who cares how people live, if living's all they got?' There is a reference to Sullivan Ballou, a Union officer in the American Civil War, who penned a famously stirring unsent letter to his wife. Perhaps the narrator is pondering a second American Civil War. At the end of the song, they turn to the heavens for reassurance that never comes:

There's got to be a better way
To talk to God and hear her say
'There are reasons why it is this way'

And with that, the album comes to an abrupt and disquieting close.

Fear Of The Dawn (2022)

Personnel:

Jack White: vocals, guitar, bass, drums, piano, synthesisers, percussion, theremin, vibraphone

With:

Dominic Davis: bass

Duane Denison: guitar

Olivia Jean: guitar

Daru Jones: drums

Jack Lawrence: bass

Bone Dust Mancini: 1975 Harley-Davidson Ironhead

Quincy McCrary: electronic piano, organ, synthesiser, harmony vocals

Q-Tip: vocals, handclaps

Mark Watrous: synthesiser

Scarlett White: bass

Producer: Jack White

Recorded at Third Man, Nashville, Tennessee, 2021

Release date: 8 April 2022

Chart places: US: 4, UK: 1, Aus: 25

All tracks written by Jack White, except where noted.

After a couple of years of rare silence, in which his only releases were retrospectives (see 'Compilations'), Jack announced not one but two new albums. If *Help Us Stranger* saw Jack return to familiar ground to regain his footing; he was now ready to take another big swing. According to an interview in *Mojo*, he was 'inspired' by the COVID-19 lockdowns:

> The lockdown was as if someone had broken my leg and I had to be laid up for six weeks. Wow, thank you for breaking my leg! Now, I'm going to write things down I wouldn't ever have written down before.

He signalled the start of this new phase with a new look: bright, dyed blue hair.

Fear Of The Dawn and its follow-up *Entering Heaven Alive* are 'companion albums', which are distinct from the more familiar double album format. In the age of streaming, when digital space is boundless and albums can be as long as (un)necessary, the double album has become a retro affectation. So, companion albums are an interesting alternative. When an artist releases two distinct, separate albums in a short timeframe, they either complement each other (like *Use Your Illusion I & II* by Guns N' Roses) or contrast with and comment on each other (like *Deliverance & Damnation* by Opeth). Jack White's albums follow the latter format: this first album is his most experimental yet, while the next is his first (almost) all-acoustic album. By releasing them both in the same year, Jack invites us to ponder the breadth and depth of his skills. And Jack had reason to be especially proud of this album, as, again, he played most of the instruments himself.

According to an interview with *Guitar Player*, Jack's mandate for this album was, 'If we're going to do it, let's do it'. He said:

> I'd like to think that *Fear Of The Dawn* is the best guitar playing that I've ever done. While mixing it and listening to the playback, I felt that I had done more with guitar on this album than anything before. I've taken my ideas further. I've experimented and taken a lot of risks with both my playing and my tone, and even with the dynamics, from very quiet to very, very loud.

Fear Of The Dawn sounds like what Jack wanted *Boarding House Reach* to be: an album that mixes classic rock with contemporary sounds and state-of-the-art production. This succeeds where its predecessor fell short because of stronger songs, fewer self-indulgent detours and a (relatively) more organic sound. That said, it's still liable to frighten non-converts and provide ammunition for Jack's many critics, who would still prefer him to return to the garage style and bash out some three-chord punk blues. This album throws out so many ideas in quick succession that it is almost too much to take in in one sitting. I would compare it to Todd Rundgren's 1973 epic *A Wizard, A True Star* – a brilliant album, but not one you'd use to make the case for the artist's greatness to the unconvinced.

'Taking Me Back'
Fear of the dawn? More like 'fear of another *Boarding House Reach*'. But fans' fears were allayed by a blistering three-chord riff in the classic Jack style, kicking off a classic Jack-style song. While the instruments are arguably just as overtly processed and electronically manipulated as they were on the last album, the overall sound is less off-puttingly artificial. Even as synths stutter and blurt, and guitar lines like angry hornets buzz past, it still sounds like a song made by humans.

Lyrically, as well, Jack, the swaggering rock god, is back. He arrogantly taunts an ex-lover who he knows is not over him – she'll be 'taking him back' before long. You could read the chorus phrase as a coded message to the fans: this song is 'taking us back' to Jack's classic hard-rockin' days. But, honestly, the lyrics don't seem that deep. When Jack tries to rhyme 'mystics' with 'picnics', it's a sign to turn off your brain and just headbang.

This was the first single, backed by the alternate version, 'Taking Me Back (Gently)', from the following album. The single edit has a hard end, while the album version segues into ...

'Fear Of The Dawn'
... this short yet powerful title track. Why does Jack fear the dawn? It seems from the lyrics – just three verses, no chorus – that he wants to linger in

the darkness with his lover as long as he can. This song is over in a rush; it functions more as a coda to the opener. The driving bass line is similar to the guitar riff on the 2005 song 'Woman' by Aussie retro-rockers Wolfmother – which, in turn, was indebted to Uriah Heep's 1972 classic 'Easy Livin'.

'The White Raven'
This impressionistic song lurches between bombastic fuzz rock and a more introspective tone. It is bookended by a hesitant guitar figure, but the main motif is an enormous recurring bass riff that grows ever more distorted as the song continues. The best moment comes when the backing vocals mimic it. Jack sings with maximum authority, although his lyrics are inscrutable. He seems to boast of his ability to switch musical genres with ease, without regard for what others think:

> My uniform is invisible
> My camouflage is invisible
> I dip my hands into sand and I'm visible
> Sewing leaves onto my skin and my material
> My motives are invisible
> My armour is invincible

'Hi-De-Ho' (Jack White, Kamaal Fareed, Cab Calloway, Buster Harding, Jack Palmer)
Coming almost full circle, Jack returns to Cab Calloway for inspiration. Only, this time, we hear the man himself singing, as the opening voice is sampled from Calloway's 1943 song 'Hi De Ho Man'. That song was based on Calloway's greatest hit 'Minnie The Moocher', which featured his iconic 'Hi-di hi-di hi-di ho' call-and-response refrain, as seen in *The Blues Brothers*. The Calloway sample ends with him saying, 'Say, Jack, ain't you glad you dug my jive?' That turns this song into a kind of call-and-response between Calloway in the past and Jack in the present.

The sample is not this song's only postmodern twist. Jack completes his embrace of hip-hop by including an actual rap artist. Kamaal Fareed, aka Q-Tip, was a member of A Tribe Called Quest, one of the greatest hip-hop groups of the 1990s. They were part of the 'Native Tongues' collective, which also included the Jungle Brothers, De La Soul, Queen Latifah and Monie Love. These artists all made music that, in contrast to the emerging gangsta rap sound of the time, was socially progressive, bright and fun, and which cleverly utilised jazz and classic rock samples. Q-Tip had been a fan of Jack's music since *De Stijl*, and when A Tribe Called Quest reunited to record an album in 2016, Jack was one of their many collaborators (see 'Collaborations & Guest Appearances'). Q-Tip repaid his work with this song.

After a gloomy introduction, with the guitar groaning as if Tony Iommi just lost another finger, a clipped P-Funk style beat starts up for Q-Tip to rap over. His lyrics use the phrase 'hi-de-ho' as a stand-in for 'mojo' or 'juice' – the charismatic power that Calloway had. He also references other examples of Black excellence: musicians Chuck Berry and Stevie Wonder, singers Minnie Riperton and Mariah Carey and basketballers Hakeem Olajuwom, LeBron James and Joel Embiid. The overall idea is that 'the Calloway vibe' is an innate force that anyone can tap into: 'Everybody got it in 'em, find yours and succeed'.

Jack occasionally pops up like he's trying to crash the song, and keeps getting cut off before he finishes his lines! Despite this song being driven entirely by a guest artist, it became a live fixture on his tour, with the rap played over the speakers while Jack plays guitar.

'Eosophobia'
This is the album's other title track, as 'eosophobia' refers to a fear of daylight. Perhaps Jack is role-playing as a vampire. Or, more likely, the lyrics are metaphorical. Consider these lines:

The sun goes down when I tell it to
But the sun comes up when it wants to

If we think about how the sun is usually used as a symbol of happiness, then perhaps Jack feels in control when he is sad, but not when he is happy, which sounds like someone grappling with bipolar disorder.

Musically, this song is just as fascinating due to Jack's incorporation of yet another musical idiom into his sound: reggae. The list of good white reggae songs is short and not especially distinguished, but the opening of this song, featuring Daru Jones' skittering drums, is a decent example, as it resembles the insouciant dub vibes of The Clash's mighty *Sandinista!* more than the forced jollity of Led Zeppelin's 'D'yer Mak'er'. The reggae section quickly gives way, however, to a rave-up based on different arrangements of the same riff, including, near the climax, a fluttering style almost like U2's The Edge.

'Into The Twilight' (Jack White, John Gillespie, Frank Paparelli, Jon Hendricks, Jay Graydon, Alan Paul)
If you thought 'Hi-De-Ho' was the oddest Jack track, you ain't heard nothin' yet! This song is a Frankenstein's Monster cobbled together from warped samples and electronically altered instruments. There's even a Vocaloid voice synthesiser: he uses a guitar pedal to translate his signal into the voice of Japanese virtual pop star Hatsune Miku. There are multiple samples from jazz vocal group The Manhattan Transfer: the opening babble of voices is from 'Another Night In Tunisia', as is the vocalese from Bobby McFerrin and scatting from Jon Hendricks; and the phrase, 'Here in the twilight', comes from 'Twilight Zone/Twilight Tone' – a song based on the opening of Rod

Sterling's *Twilight Zone* TV show! There is also a spoken word excerpt from beat poet William Burroughs that summarises Jack's current ethos: 'When you cut into the present, the future leaks out'.

Jack's voice is heard only as part of the mass chorus, which aims to reassure us: 'Here in the night, everything's right'. But is it? The song feels like a dream where you're falling through a 1950s industrial musical movie (like General Motors' *Design For Dreaming*), where commercial jingles, space-age pop and garage rock have merged into an amorphous *Akira*-style cyborg. This is the real '21st Century Blues'.

'Dusk'

Jack kicks off side two with a lovely 30-second guitar instrumental that brings to mind the Genesis song of the same name, evoking the meditative melancholy that comes over one during the gloaming.

'What's The Trick'

After a handful of experimental tracks, Jack returns to more conventional territory with a paint-stripping riff and an imperious vocal. But watch out! The song is interrupted by a motorcycle sound 'played' by the awesomely named Bone Dust Mancini. This is followed by a hip-hop-style break, then an even more distorted version of the riff. As he burrows down through layers of distortion towards a warped vocoder climax, Jack grapples with his own motives for doing what he does:

This is my first
My worst
My past
And my last
Imperfect effort

He has to balance his quality control with his innate drive to be relentlessly productive:

If I die tomorrow
What did I do today?

The key line (and the funniest moment on a very funny album) is 'Plus one and minus one equals zero. That's a defeatist attitude!' Is Jack railing against the very nature of reality itself? No, he is simply refusing to adopt a 'zero-sum' attitude – to act as if there is a limited amount of time and resources, and every action comes with an opportunity cost. One has to wonder how his attitude was affected by growing up in Detroit, as the phrase, 'Gentlemen of elegant appearance in a state of bustitude', references a dissertation by Shirley Diana Hunter Smith, from Purdue University, about

113

the industrialisation of the Midwest. And who said rock music can't teach you anything?

'That Was Then, This Is Now'

This is the song on the album most reminiscent of Jack's early work, with a big singalong chorus and a cocky riff halfway between strut and swing. But lest we get too comfortable, the title phrase ushers in an arresting funk-trash riff and Jack snarls out the lyrics, which are sparse in concrete detail, but seem to be about the loss of childhood certainties.

'Eosophobia (Reprise)'

The spidery 'Eosophobia' riff returns, ushering in a heavy jam session with the band. The opening is the closest Jack has come to Joe Satriani-style shredding. The minimal lyrics are a cocky extension of the original song's theme:

You think the sun listens to no one
But you're wrong
It listens to me!

But Jack sounds like he's trying to convince himself that he has things under control.

'Morning, Noon And Night'

This is one of the few songs on this album with a memorable lyrical melody. The lyrics may not be especially interesting – it's a song of seduction, with further mentions of lost childhood innocence and fairy tales – but Jack sells them with one of his most convincing vocal performances in a while. The key to this song's success, compared to the pre-fab likes of 'Connected By Love', is that this never sounds ironic or detached. The music has a marching beat, similar to 'Five To One' by The Doors, and is driven along by burbling keyboard trills reminiscent of Giorgio Moroder's *Neverending Story* score. The fake-out ending features the same guitar figure as 'Dusk'. This song also features the first guitar solo on any Jack album not played by the man himself! Dwayne Denison, the former guitarist of noise rockers The Jesus Lizard, plays the solo, and that came about because his daughter was friends with Jack's daughter Scarlet!

'Shedding My Velvet'

The final song is one of the low-key highlights of the album. Jack plays all the instruments, and his choice of electric piano and bluesy guitar makes this feel like a vulnerable personal statement. The vibe is again similar to U2's original version of 'Love Is Blindness'. However, this song does not see Jack making grand, sweeping statements about love. Instead, he lays bare his insecurity:

I'm not as bad as I was, but I'm not as good
As I can be, as I can be

And also his arrogance:

The noblesse oblige you sense is mine
When I convey my lines
'Better to illuminate than merely to shine'

In the same song, Jack admits that he feels like he has not lived up to his potential, while also styling himself as an aristocrat lighting the way for the less fortunate. The latter is fair enough, given the success of Third Man Records, but it is, nevertheless, a brazen thing to admit in song, when the new default for modern rock stars is to be artificially humble. After so much bluster and posturing, it is nice to catch a glimpse of Jack, the fallible human. The soft acoustic coda is like a graceful bow that points the way to the companion album.

Entering Heaven Alive (2022)

Personnel:
Jack White: vocals, guitar, bass, drums, percussion, piano, organ, electric piano, vibraphone, drum machine, Mellotron, synthesiser
Dominic Davis: bass
Dean Fertita: electric piano
Olivia Jean: guitar, bass, percussion, shakers
Daru Jones: drums
Fats Kaplin: violin, viola, strings
Patrick Keeler: drums
Pokey LaFarge: guitar
Jack Lawrence: bass
Dan Mancini: guitar
Quincy McCrary: piano
Ben Swank: drums
Mark Watrous: piano, keys, electric piano
Cory Younts: piano
Producer: Jack White
Recorded at Third Man, Nashville, Tennessee, 2021
Release date: 22 July 2022
Chart places: US: 9, UK: 4, Aus: 43
All tracks written by Jack White

Jack's second album of 2022 was a tonic for people turned off by the overt artificiality of *Fear Of The Dawn*. These are all mostly acoustic songs, and their arrangements put more emphasis on Jack's lyrics and singing. Therefore, it made sense for him to release these songs as a separate package, as combining these and *Fear Of The Dawn* into one platter would have been like mixing oil and whisky. However, grouping these songs together has resulted in an album that feels monotonous. There are some interesting sounds within the individual songs, but they all blur together on a cursory listen.

It is probable that this album's generally pleasant and contended vibe was due to Jack's relationship with his guitarist Olivia Jean. He proposed to her on stage during a concert on 8 April 2022, and they were married on stage!

The title refers to a religious doctrine – in Catholicism and other belief systems – that certain, especially holy people can be taken to Heaven without experiencing physical death. The cover is a black-and-white photo of a woman working a loom. The old-timey symbolism makes it seem as if Jack is getting back in touch with that 'Old Weird America' that has always been at the heart of his music.

'A Tip From You To Me'

This opens with a quote from British philosopher John Stuart Mill, one of the key figures in classical liberal politics and utilitarian ethics: 'Ask yourself if you are happy and then you cease to be'. Jack seems to be questioning his own well-being, specifically whether he wants to be alone or not. The lyrics shift between first and third person, making it hard to tell what his final conclusion is. The vocal melody, with his moans and groans, is reminiscent of Robert Plant circa *Led Zeppelin III*. The music is a top-notch folk band performance, with Mark Watrous' dramatic piano lines being the highlight.

'All Along The Way'
This opens with Jack singing quietly, accompanied only by his acoustic guitar, before the full band join in. Except that there is no band, as Jack plays all the instruments, except for additional guitar and bass by Olivia Jean. It's a pleasant reverie of a song as Jack reflects on romances past. He concludes that people in love leave 'clues' for each other: 'We're not dumb, we'll leave crumbs, all along the way'.

'Help Me Along'
A lovely string introduction leads into a bouncy Wurlitzer riff. The third verse adds vibes (played by Jack) to the mix, which gives the music a jaunty feel. This song has a warm and inviting sound reminiscent of mid-1960s British folk-pop of the more straitlaced variety, such as Cat Stevens. It also features some of Jack's most unabashedly vulnerable lyrics, as he opens his heart to his lover, pledging to help her, and pre-emptively begging for forgiveness. The final verse is practically a wedding vow:

If you'll let me belong to you for richer or poorer
Let me belong to you for all that you're worth
Though the ties may unravel for the worse or for better
You should know that I'll travel to the ends of the earth

'Love Is Selfish'
With just Jack on acoustic guitar and bass, plus gentle brushes and washes of cymbals, this harkens back to the simplicity of The White Stripes. Jack ponders the nature of love: 'It's always crying, 'Me, me, me'', he sings. As on 'Help Me Along', Jack seems to be pre-emptively trying to make his partner understand his flaws. When he gets caught up in romance, he does not feel in control:

I'm on a train, but I can not rest upon it
I'm on a train, but it won't stay on the rails
And I got a sailboat with her name painted on it
But I don't know how to sail

'I've Got You Surrounded (With My Love)'
This low-key funk jam sticks out like a sore thumb after four acoustic-based songs. The electric guitar and drum machine disrupt the pastoral mood. The

percussion, in general, sounds like something Jack found in Tom Waits' leftovers draw. The lyrics are just variations on the title; Jack's goofiest boast yet. But there's a fatalistic twist in the bridge: 'Falling down with you, we trip and fall together'.

'Queen Of The Bees'
More jaunty folk-pop. The rolling marimba is, again, very Tom Waits-like, as is the recurring blurt like an elephant's trumpet. When the organ solo starts up, with added marimba, it shifts into more of a Martin Denny exotica vibe. The lyrics are interesting, as Jack pledges his love via a variety of laboured similes (the pick-up being, 'I wanna hold you like a sloth hugs a tree') before concluding that he and his partner might as well be different species: 'I'm a fly on the wall and you're the queen of the bees'.

'A Tree On Fire From Within'
The opening lyrics frame this as a story song, but there's no apparent narrative. Jack seems to be imploring us to reach out to people who may be in need of emotional support. The title phrase is a metaphor for inner turmoil that does not show on the surface. In line with the insular theme of the song, Jack plays all the instruments. For a change, the bass is practically the lead instrument, and Jack's dexterous playing is impressive.

'If I Die Tomorrow'
This song has a portentous title and a melody to match. The lyrics start by indulging that common neurotic fantasy of attending one's own funeral to hear what people really thought of you, and conclude with Jack taking stock of how much he owes the people who have loved him. Once again, he plays all the instruments, and the seams are a little more hearable here. The drums sound somewhat stiff, as if sampled, and there is a stuttering buzzing noise in the bridge. By far, the highlight of the song is the Mellotron, another obsolete instrument that defined a particular era in rock – in this case, early 1970s prog.

This was released as a digital single, with a cinematic video about a man dragging a coffin through a frozen post-apocalyptic wilderness.

'Please God, Don't Tell Anyone'
Jack continues in confessional mode, except now he plays the part of a robber who worries that his sins will be exposed when his family reach Heaven. The lyrics contend with a classic Christian moral quandary: even if he started stealing for the sake of his weeping children, a sin is still a sin in the eyes of God. Underpinning this is the social construct that a man must be the breadwinner: 'Oh, baby, what have I done? Have I proven myself to no one?' In contrast with the dark lyrics, the music is loose and limber, with a particularly delightful piano solo from Quincy McCrary.

'A Madman From Manhattan'

This title sounds like the name of an old silent comedy short, but the lyrics are serious. They tell of a dapper character who strings women along, but his behaviour is excused because of how he was treated in the past. Musically, this is the highlight of the album, as Jack tries yet another genre on for size. This has elements of Brazilian bossa nova, but it is more of a synthesis. Perhaps Jack should consider making a Tropicália album sometime. His delivery of the lyrics, filled with internal rhymes and retro slang (like the man being a 'cat' and the girl a 'dime'), brings to mind the jazz rap of the early 1990s, such as Digable Planets' 'Cool Like That'.

'Taking Me Back (Gently)'

And now Jack circles back on himself to bring his 2022 duology to a close. This has the same chord sequence as the version on *Fear Of The Dawn*, but the riff is replaced by a violin line. The instrumental bridge is lovely, with long descending piano runs and a 'wild west saloon' solo from Cory Younts, followed by a duel between Fats Kaplin's violin and Pokey LaFarge's acoustic guitar. Jack really knows how to pick great musicians. The track closes with the same feedback melody that opened *Fear Of The Dawn*; like Pink Floyd's *The Wall*, you could play these two albums on a loop.

Non-Album Tracks, B-Sides And Rarities

These are officially released studio recordings by Jack White and his bands that are available on singles, compilations and soundtracks. They are sorted chronologically by artist. Live covers and non-album live tracks are excluded, as are all demo versions released on special editions, although I have addressed particularly notable remixes and re-recordings.

The White Stripes
All tracks written by Jack White, except where noted.
'Let's Shake Hands'
This was the A-side of The White Stripes' first single: a non-album track released in March 1998 by Italy Records as a 7" vinyl. This is the prototypical White Stripes song: a simple drum beat with guitar histrionics dancing atop, and a lyric that flits between innocent friendship and romantic frustration. The track is available digitally and on the *Greatest Hits* collection, but copies of the physical single are highly sought after by collectors. According to the online database *Discogs*, one copy sold for $750. And it wasn't even the 2008 re-release with hand-stencilled art!

'Look Me Over Closely' (Terry Gilkyson)
This was the B-side of 'Let's Shake Hands'. It's a cover of a Marlene Dietrich song, first recorded in 1953 with Percy Faith & His Orchestra. Dietrich was a German actress-singer, whose epic career spanned Weimar Era silent films, Golden Age Hollywood and a travelling cabaret show where she worked with Burt Bacharach. Her brazen sexuality, distinctive accent and cutting-edge fashion made her the archetypal decadent-yet-classy 'vamp'. It's no wonder she appealed to the aesthetics-obsessed young Jack.

'Lafayette Blues'
This was the A-side of the band's second single: another non-album track, released in November 1998 by Italy Records on a 7" vinyl, with 'Sugar Never Tasted So Good' as the B-side. This track is available digitally, and also on the US CD edition of the 'Fell In Love With A Girl' single (along with 'Let's Shake Hands'). The original single is the most collectable White Stripes rarity. It was pressed on red-and-white swirled vinyl, and around 15 copies had hand-painted covers by Jack and Dave Buick (the owner of Italy Records). Jack also apparently inserted some French franc notes inside some copies for a lark, and handed these out to friends at a release show. In the song, Jack shouts out Detroit streets with French names. It's a gimmick song, but there's great double-tracked guitar twiddling.

'Red Bowling Ball Ruth'
This was the B-side of 'The Big Three Killed My Baby'. It's a fun but incoherent basher about the title character breaking her tooth on a bowling

ball ... and Saint Peter is there, too? This is the definition of musical juvenilia. The red bowling ball of the title reappears in 'Hand Springs'.

'Hand Springs'

This is about a man throwing a tantrum in a bowling alley when a suave pinball player steals his girl away. It was one side of a split 7" with The Dirtbombs, released in 2000 as a free gift with the pinball fanzine *Multiball*. It was also included on the compilation *Hot Pinball Rock, Vol. 1*. It is not surprising that garage rock fans would also be pinball aficionados. Both garage rock and pinball originated in an era before youth culture was fully commodified and sold back to us. If only The White Stripes had a song about hot rods, they would hit the trifecta of modern retro-rockabilly obsessions. In 2012, this song was repackaged, with 'Red Death At 6:14' on the flip side, as a special release for Record Store Day.

'Jolene' (Dolly Parton)

The studio version of this cover was the B-side of 'Hello Operator' and is included on the *Greatest Hits* collection. The more well-known live version was released in 2004 to promote the *Under Blackpool Lights* DVD.

This is The White Stripes' most famous cover version, and one of the most significant cover songs released by a rock band in the 2000s. It was not as if rock fans were unaware of the brilliance of Dolly Parton, but for Gen X, at least, she was more of a kitsch icon, known for pop-county bops like '9 To 5' and 'Islands In The Stream'. This cover directed the youngsters' attention to her iconic self-penned 1970s work. It helped that it's a distinctive rendition, which replaces Dolly's forlorn resignation about the titular woman out to steal her man, with a violent stop-start arrangement. Jack sounds like he's on the verge of a psychotic break, as he begs Jolene to leave them alone.

This cover was also instrumental in re-contextualising Jack's career, demonstrating how he was influenced as much by country as by blues, and, thus, it laid the groundwork for his work with Loretta Lynn. The key was that he played this cover completely straight. There's no winking at the audience as if it was beneath a 'cool' rock band to cover a song by music's most famous self-proclaimed bimbo. *NME*'s Stevie Chick said: 'There was nothing ironic about it, in the era when every shitty indie band did an ironic Britney Spears cover'. Their sincerity was refreshing. As was the fact that Jack didn't switch up the pronouns. Jack said to the *Metro-Times*: 'I love putting myself from [sic] the female standpoint. Especially in my own songwriting... it's a great way to jump out of your body and look at it from a different point of view'. This also made the cover a stealth queer statement, if one were inclined to read it that way.

'Lord, Send Me An Angel' (William Samuel McTell)

This was the A-side of a non-album single released in 2000. It's a cover of a Blind Willie McTell song, wherein the narrator boasts of his sexual conquests, comparing them based on their place of origin, skin tone and marital status. It is, to put it charitably, not in tune with today's more sensitive racial and sexual mores. The only lyrics Jack changed were the specific place names, which was either very brave or very stupid of him. According to an interview with *Mojo*, in recording such an over-the-top piece of braggadocio, he was making fun of himself.

'You're Pretty Good Looking' ('Trendy American' remix)
This was the B-side of 'Lord Send Me An Angel'. The 'remix' is a joke, as the only change is that Jack's voice is occasionally distorted as if by vocoder – as was popular in American dance-pop at the time, e.g. Cher and Madonna.

'Party Of Special Things To Do' (Don Van Vliet, Elliot Ingber)
'China Pig' (Don Van Vliet)
'Ashtray Heart' (Don Van Vliet)
These three songs were released on a 7" in 2000 as part of the Sub Pop Records singles club. At the time, Sub Pop were one of the many labels looking at Detroit as the 'new Seattle'. The Go signed with them and The White Stripes might have followed suit if Jack had not been canny. He wanted to contribute to Sub Pop's legendary single club, but he noted in the contract that the label would have owned the rights to the songs. Hence, he recorded three cover versions instead.

These songs are all by the iconic art-rocker Captain Beefheart. The first is from his unloved 1974 'sell-out' album *Bluejeans & Moonbeams*, the second is from the legendary 1969 double album/endurance test *Trout Mask Replica* and the third is from Beefheart's second 'comeback' album, 1980's *Doc At The Radar Station*. With his seven-octave vocal range, surreal lyrics and dense musical arrangements, Captain Beefheart is not the easiest artist to cover. But Jack was ready to show the full range of his influences and make it clear he was not some trad-blues revivalist. Besides, under all the shifting time signatures, the blues was at the heart of Beefheart's sound, going back to his debut album *Safe As Milk*, with Ry Cooder on guitar. In a canny move, Jack personally sent copies of these to Beefheart fan John Peel, thus netting him some radio airplay.

'Hotel Yorba' (live version)
This was released as a single in the UK. Jack, Meg and Brendan Benson snuck into the titular hotel to record this campfire singalong version, as well as its B-side.

'Rated X' (Loretta Lynn)
This cover of Loretta Lynn's 1972 song was the B-side of the UK live 'Hotel Yorba' single. The song is about the sexist way divorced women are treated, an unusual topic for a divorced man in a band with his ex-wife to sing about.

But Jack's rendition was good enough that, when Lynn heard it, she allowed Jack to work with her, and the rest is history (see 'Productions').

'Love Sick' (Bob Dylan)
This live cover was a B-side of the UK 'Fell In Love With A Girl' CD single. This song was the opening cut on Dylan's incredible 1997 comeback album *Time Out Of Mind*. It's a lumbering mutant blues with a gothic vibe, ideally suited for The White Stripes. Jack – playing guitar and organ – dug beneath Daniel Lanois' densely layered production to find the tortured torch song buried there.

'Red Death At 6:14'
This is from the 2001 *Sympathetic Sounds Of Detroit* compilation (see 'Productions'), and was re-released in 2012 for Record Store Day as the B-side of 'Hand Springs'. It's a slight but catchy bash-around about a dead girl. What '6:14' refers to is unknown; most fans speculate it's a Bible verse.

'Candy Cane Children'
This was originally released in 1998 on a Christmas-themed 7" single called *Surprise Package Volume 2* on the Flying Bomb label, alongside songs by Rocket 455 and The Blowtops. It is more commonly available on a 2002 single released by XL. The cover of that single is a priceless photo of Jack and Meg selling 'Christmas cheer', as with a children's lemonade stand.

The non-album Christmas single is a tradition running from The Beatles to Pearl Jam to, uh, The Darkness. Jack continues the tradition of Christmas songs being real bummers, as this one concerns a girl and a boy who are alone at Christmas. Jack doesn't even try to offer comfort; quite the opposite: 'And you think it might be fun to get a new toy. Think again, boy'.

'The Story Of The Magi / Silent Night'
The B-side of 'Candy Cane Children' sees Jack reading from the Gospel of St. Matthew, and Meg singing the carol 'Silent Night'. Jack and Meg argue about a famous mondegreen (misheard lyric): 'Round John Virgin'. This is for completists only.

'Baby Blue' (Gene Vincent, Bobby Jones)
After John Peel enthused about rockabilly legend Gene Vincent to Jack and Meg over dinner., they recorded this song for a Peel session in 2001, helping ensure that their sessions got healthy play on his radio show.

'Good To Me' (Brendan Benson, Jason Faulkner)
This cover of a Brendan Benson song was a B-side of 'Seven Nation Army' in 2003. It was another step on the road to The Raconteurs. The song's co-writer, Jason Faulkner, is a talented rock journeyman, best known (by cool people) for his work in the ace early-1990s power pop band Jellyfish.

'Black Jack Davey' (traditional)

This was a B-side on the 'Seven Nation Army' CD and digital single. It is a cover of a traditional folk tune dating back 300 years to Scotland, where it was originally called 'The Raggle Taggle Gypsy'. It has been recorded by just about every folk artist of note, from The Carter Family and Woody Guthrie, to Shirley Collins and Bob Dylan. While the words have changed over time, the basic story, about a woman running away to join her lover in the travelling people, has remained the same. The White Stripes' version features some fantastic galloping guitar from Jack.

'Who's To Say...' (Dan Miller)

This was a B-Side on the 'I Just Don't Know What to Do With Myself' CD single. It is a cover of a song by alt-county band Blanche, a spin-off of Goober & The Peas. Jack played slide on the original, which Brendan Benson also played on.

'St. Ides Of March' (Ben Swank, Johnny Walker)

This was the B-side of 'The Hardest Button To Button. It is a cover of a song by the Soledad Brothers (named after a group of convicted Black Panther members). Meg was dating one member, Henry Oliver, at the time. Another member, Johnny Walker, played slide guitar on The White Stripes' debut and taught Jack to play slide. The third member, Ben Swank, co-founded Third Man Records and plays on *Entering Heaven Alive*.

'Blue Orchid' (High Contrast remix)

This remix by Welsh DJ High Contrast is a full-on dance version mixing drum'n'bass beats and dubstep low-end. As far as dance remixes of rock songs go, this is a quality example of a deathly subgenre.

'Who's A Big Baby?'

This was a B-side on one edition of the 'Blue Orchid' UK CD single. It must be the most lyrically insubstantial Jack White song of all time. It's certainly the most irritating, due to the distorted whiny vocal. Patrick Keeler is credited for 'Shhhshing and assisting'.

'Though I Hear You Calling, I Will Not Answer'

This was a B-side on the other edition of the 'Blue Orchid' UK CD single. It's a minor song, with more annoying distorted vocals. There's also more marimba, if you're a fan.

'Shelter Of Your Arms' (Craig Fox)

This cover of a song by The Greenhornes was the B-side of 'The Denial Twist'. It is also available on the Japanese edition of the 'Walking With A Ghost' EP.

'Walking With A Ghost' (Sara Quin, Tegan Quin)

This song was released in 2005 as a non-album CD single in different editions, either with just this song or with live cuts. It is a cover of a 2004 tune by Canadian twin sister act Tegan & Sara. It's a neat song about feeling haunted by your ex, with a compelling metaphorical hook: 'I was walking with a ghost, I said please, please don't exist'. Compare this to 'Little Ghost'.

It is unusual for Jack to cover a song by a contemporary act, especially one with no Detroit affiliation, so he must have really liked this song. The White Stripes' riff-tastic rendition is a far cry from the original's twee-folk style, and it remains one of the band's best-kept secrets. It is not even available to stream.

'Top Special'

This song was recorded at Dave Feeny's studio and sold as a limited edition 3" one-sided vinyl single during the 2005-6 UK tour. It was sold alongside special mini-turntables that the band had purchased in bulk from their Japanese manufacturer. The turntables can fetch high prices on the collectors market, despite only being able to play this single and 3" re-releases of select White Stripes singles.

If you're too lazy and disrespectful to spend up to $1000 buying one of these singles and a mini turntable to play it on, like a REAL FAN would, then you can hear this song on YouTube. With Jack's voice warped into a high pitch, plus the massed backing vocals, this sounds like a theme from some demented old children's program.

'Baby Brother' (Vern Orr)

This was the B-side of the 'Icky Thump' single and is also available on the Japanese edition of *Icky Thump* and the iTunes pre-order edition. The White Stripes turned this 1959 rockabilly tune by Bill Carter And The Rovin' Gamblers into a rollicking Misfits-style thrasher. The narrator lives in fear of his sinister baby brother, who he insists can crawl on the walls and swim in the goldfish bowl. If it had been written by Jack, it could be considered a sequel to 'The Hardest Button To Button'.

'Tennessee Border' (Jimmy Work)

This live cover of a song made famous by Hank Williams was a bonus track (along with 'Baby Brother') on the iTunes pre-order edition. It's hard to screw up a Hank Williams heartbreak song – and they don't.

'You Don't Know What Love Is (You Just Do As You're Told)' (acoustic version)

This was a B-side of the original song. In my opinion, this is one White Stripes song that does not work with an acoustic arrangement.

'You Don't Know What Love Is (You Just Do As You're Told)' (Frat Rock version)

This was another B-side on the CD single of the original song. What makes it a 'frat rock' version is apparently the replacement of the guitar with an organ. The frat guys I knew as a teen listened to Limp Bizkit and Blink-182, so times have apparently changed.

'A Martyr For My Love For You' (acoustic version)

This was the B-side on the 7" single 'You Don't Know What Love Is'. It's a hushed and spooky version, somewhat similar to Donovan.

'Conquest' (acoustic mariachi version) (Corky Robbins)

The red vinyl 7" single of 'Conquest' has this version in place of the original. The acoustic arrangement makes this cover feel slightly more authentic – not like proper mariachi music mind; more like a song from a 1940s Tex-Mex-themed musical.

This is also available as the B-side of the Spanish language version. This was recorded in the living room of indie rocker Beck, as were the following three B-sides.

'It's My Fault For Being Famous'

This was the B-side on the black 7" 'Conquest' single. This song is one of Jack's most overt screeds against pushy fans and snooping journalists. Beck contributes piano and backing vocals.

'Honey, We Can't Afford To Look This Cheap'

This was the B-side of the white 7" 'Conquest' single. It is a fun song inspired by Jack's move to Nashville, where he was afraid of looking low-rent compared to Music City residents. Full of cute details and self-deprecating humour, this is one of Jack's best non-album tracks. Beck contributes the intermittent slide guitar. This is also available on the *Acoustic Recordings* compilation.

'Cash Grab Complications On The Matter'

This was the B-side on the red 7" 'Conquest' single. 'The Whole Crew' (presumably the musicians that recorded the acoustic version of 'Conquest') are credited with 'stompin' and clappin'. This is a love song with shades of the myth of Narcissus, by way of *Pygmalion*: 'What gave me this power to construct you?'

'Conquista' (Corky Robbins)

This is the album version of 'Conquest' with a re-recorded Spanish-language vocal track. It was released as a single in 2008, with the acoustic 'Conquest' on the B-side.

'Signed D.C.' (Arthur Lee)
This and the following song were released as a vinyl single in 2011 as a Third Man Records 'From the Vault' exclusive. It is a cover of a 1966 song by cult Californian band Love. It is a murky version that fails to capture Arthur Lee's spooky grace.

'I've Been Loving You Too Long' (Jerry Butler, Otis Redding)
They give it a good try, but let's just say that they don't live up to Otis Redding's 1965 original – but that is an unfair standard to live up to.

'City Lights'
This was released on the Jack White *Acoustic Recordings* compilation. It was written for *Get Behind Me Satan* in 2005 but was not finished until 2016. It is a pleasant, if slightly overwrought and meandering love ballad. The title might have been inspired by the Charlie Chaplin film of the same name, but the lyrics have a more modern co-dependent sensibility.

The Raconteurs
'Steady, As She Goes' (acoustic version) (Benson, White)
This version was the A-side of a vinyl single and was also included as a B-side on the Australia CD single.

 The arrangement is more or less the same, except that it goes into swing time for the chorus, and there is some sparkling acoustic playing in between verses, reminiscent of Funkadelic's 'Can You Get To That'. You can hear Jack and Benson laughing in the lead-up to the final chorus, swept up in the joie de vivre of their new band.

'The Bane Rendition' (Benson, White)
This was the B-side of the 'Steady, As She Goes' CD single. It is an instrumental jam based around a riff that's practically identical to 'La Grange' by ZZ Top, which, in turn, means it's a direct descendent of John Lee Hooker's immortal 'Boogie Chillen''. It has neither the roof-raising power of the former nor the menace of the latter, but it's a pleasant enough listen.

'It Ain't Easy' (Ron Davies)
This live recording was a B-Side of the live 'Hands' vinyl single. It's a cover of a 1970 song by American songwriter Ron Davies, which most people would know of via David Bowie's rendition on his epochal *Ziggy Stardust* album, where it sticks out like a sore thumb.

 It's a solid song, though, and Benson does justice to the melody, even if the band sound underpowered. If you want to hear a proper gutbucket blues take on this song, check out Long John Baldry's 1971 version with Ron Wood on guitar.

'Headin' For The Texas Border' (Cyril Jordan, Roy Loney)
This was the B-side on the 'Broken Boy Soldier' studio version vinyl single. It is a live cover of a Flamin' Groovies song from 1970. Flamin' Groovies were one of the great cult bands of the 70s, who straddled blues rock, proto-punk and power pop. This song is on the punkier end of the spectrum, and The Raconteurs play it hard and fast, with a ripping guitar solo from Jack. But the original is still tops. Raconteurs fans owe it to themselves to check out Flamin' Groovies albums *Teenage Head* and *Shake Some Action*, which sound like alternative rock before that was even a concept.

'Top Yourself' (bluegrass version) (Benson, White)
This was the B-Side of 'Salute Your Solution' and is also available on the *Acoustic Recordings* compilation. This is arguably superior to the album version, as you can discern more clearly the tasty contributions from Benson on mandolin, Lawrence on banjo and Dirk Powell on fiddle.

'Carolina Drama' (acoustic version)
Also from the *Acoustic Recordings* compilation, this stripped-down arrangement, with extra violin, makes this song feel even more like an old folk tale passed down over generations.

'Many Shades Of Black' (with Adele on vocals) (Benson, White)
This was the B-side of this song's single release, and it is also available on the deluxe edition of Adele's debut album *19*. As the queen of melodramatic break-up songs for wine mums to wail along with, this song was a natural fit for Adele. While the music is the same, her retro-soul stylings give the song a more timeless feel; you could imagine it on the soundtrack of a Swinging Sixties film starring Michael Caine and Diana Rigg.

'Old Enough' (bluegrass version) (Benson, White, Boudleaux Bryant, Felice Bryant)
This was released as a CD and vinyl single, separate from the album version. This features Ricky Skaggs on mandolin and Ashley Monroe on vocals. Skaggs is a modern bluegrass legend, one of the so-called 'new traditionalists' who helped revitalise country music in the 1980s after the dead-end of the 'urban cowboy' pop country mini-boom. In many ways, Skaggs was to country in the 1980s what Jack was to blues in the 2000s.

Monroe is a country singer-songwriter who debuted in 2006 but managed to avoid being ground into electro-pop slush by the modern Nashville music machine. She makes rootsy country music both on her own and in the supergroup Pistol Annies, with Miranda Lambert and Angaleena Presley. She also contributed backing vocals on the album Jack produced for Wanda Jackson, *The Party Ain't Over* (see 'Productions') and released her own *Live At Third Man Records* album.

This guest pair bring authenticity and timeless class to this song. There is an extended breakdown showcasing Skaggs' delicate playing. He trades licks with Jack's acoustic guitar, before the band segue into the chorus of The Everly Brothers' 'Wake Up Little Susie'. At the climax, Monroe's vocals blend with the boys' for some pleasingly ragged four-part harmonies. Dick Powell also shines; his fiddle gives the song a barn dance feel. You can see in the performance video for this single that everyone enjoyed themselves immensely.

If there was any justice in the lawless West, this should have been a massive hit. But it had to settle with being nominated for the Country Music Association Award 'Musical Event of the Year' award. Of course, it lost to the Brad Paisley & Keith Urban duet 'Start A Band', the epitome of faux-authentic, assembly-line, pop-country schlock.

'Open Your Eyes' (Benson, White)
This and the following track were recorded during the *Consolers Of The Lonely* sessions, and released as a standalone vinyl single in 2012 as part of the Third Man Records 'From The Vault' series, the only 'new' Raconteurs music for the 11 years between the second and third albums. This is a naggingly tuneful, if musically simplistic, tune reminiscent of early 1990s alt-pop like Matthew Sweet, wherein Benson's takedown of a pampered rich person is punctuated by Jack's spiky guitar solo. Benson recorded a solo version of this for his 2012 album *What Kind Of World*, where it was titled 'Here In The Deadlights' (presumably in reference to Stephen King's *It*, although I have no idea why).

'You Made A Fool Out Of Me' (Benson, White)
This song was re-recorded by Benson for his 2009 album *My Old Familiar Friend*. The Raconteurs' version sounds like a collection of ideas that didn't suit the song, but the finished version is a stately string-laden ballad.

The Dead Weather
'Are 'Friends' Electric' (Gary Numan)
This was the B-side of 'Hang You From The Heavens'. It is a cover of the Gary Numan & Tubeway Army song, a futuristic tale of android companions that was one of the first major synthpop hits in 1979. So this was an odd choice of a cover for a band seeped in blues influences. Or so you might think, because they turn this song into a mid-60s psychedelic nugget ala The Seeds, with Fertita reimagining the original's synth riff as something like a demented fairground organ.

'Treat Me Like Your Mother' (Diplo remix) (Fertita, Lawrence, Mosshart, White)
The was released as a digital single. Diplo is an American DJ who has worked with every significant modern pop and electronic act, from Madonna

and Britney Spears, to Mark Ronson and Skrillex. He reduces the song to a clattering rhythm, a swirling synth line and some chopped-and-screwed vocal interjections. It's not bad if you're into this sort of thing; it just continuously sounds like it's about to really pop off and it never does. But kudos to the band for trying something different.

'You Just Can't Win' (Van Morrison)
This was a B-side of 'Treat Me Like Your Mother'. It is a cover of a 1966 album track by Them, the Northern Irish blues rock group. Them is best known for launching the long and winding career of folk-soul-blues mystic Van Morrison. While most of Them's hits were covers, this, like their iconic garage rock staple 'Gloria', was a Morrison original. As with Jack, Morrison's early songs were loving imitations, and this is a classic blues lament that could have been written by Ray Charles. Jack sings it completely straight, which is why this cover works.

'A Child Of A Few Hours Is Burning To Death' (Bob Markley, Ron Morgan)
This was a B-side of 'Cut Like A Buffalo'. It is a cover of a song by the cult Californian psychedelic group The West Coast Pop Art Experimental Band from their 1968 album *A Child's Guide To Good And Evil*. That album, with its mix of West Coast folk-pop and acid-fried fuzz rock, is exactly the kind of forgotten almost-masterpiece that vinyl crate-diggers love to evangelise about. This song is a Vietnam protest fever dream, with images of fire and death that make '21st Century Schizoid Man' seem tame. This is a fantastic, live-sounding band performance with great bluesy lead guitar.

'Forever My Queen' (Bobby Liebling)
This was the A-side of a non-album single released in 2009. It is a cover of a song by American cult metal band Pentagram. They had no success in the mid-1970s but reunited in the 1980s, just in time to help invent doom metal. The Dead Weather version of this song is metallic, but not doomy.

'Outside' (Keith Evans, Michael O'Donnell)
This was the B-side to 'Forever My Queen', and an iTunes pre-order exclusive. It is a straightforward cover of a song by the obscure 1960s freakbeat group Downliners Sect.

'I Feel Strange' (Fertita, Lawrence, Mosshart, White)
This was contained inside the 'Blue Blood Blues' 'triple-decker' 12" vinyl, and you had to crack your copy open to get to it. As befitting such a troll move by the band, it's one of their better songs. It has a mellow groove with chunky bass, a catchy lead guitar line and a sunny yet ominous semi-acoustic breakdown for the chorus. Jack and Mosshart sing together,

pleading for help with their inner demons. The guitar tone is reminiscent of Robby Krieger, so this could be considered The Dead Weather's answer to The Doors' 'Strange Days'.

'Rolling In On A Burning Tire' (Fertita, Lawrence, Mosshart, White)
This non-album track was included on the soundtrack of the 2010 movie *The Twilight Saga: Eclipse*. Yes, that's the young adult romance series with the sparkly vampires. Say what you will about that series, their soundtracks were thoughtfully curated. As evidence, this album also includes fresh songs by Beck, The Black Keys, Muse, Vampire Weekend, Band Of Horses and Florence + The Machine. Anecdotal evidence suggests that these soundtracks provided an introduction to alt-rock for many teenage girls.

As for this song, it has more of a 'spaghetti Western meets delta blues' vibe than most of their first album. The ominous feel is suited to a vampire movie, although perhaps one more ostentatiously gothic than *Twilight*. That said, the lyric, 'Rolling in on a burning tire, you're gonna set my house on fire', fits the series' theme of uncontrollable, obsessive love.

Jack White
All songs written by Jack White unless otherwise noted.
'Wayfaring Stranger' (Traditional)
'Sitting On Top Of The World' (Lonnie Chatmon, Walter Vinson)
'Christmas Time Will Soon Be Over' (Traditional)
'Great High Mountain' (Traditional)
Jack recorded these covers for the *Cold Mountain* soundtrack. They are all traditional songs, except for 'Sitting On Top Of The World', a country blues tune from 1930 that is probably best known from Cream's 1968 version. To *Q* magazine, Jack said that this soundtrack was 'the chance to expose American folk music, which doesn't get heard'. His versions of these songs are certainly reverential. Bluegrass legend Ralph Stanley arranged the version of 'Great High Mountain'.

'Never Far Away'
This was Jack's lone original song on the *Cold Mountain* soundtrack. It's a pleasant acoustic ramble that describes the journey of the film's main character walking back to his wife. Released in 2004, this soundtrack reached number 51 on the US *Billboard* 200. It sold decently but did not become the same kind of breakout hit that the *O Brother, Where Art Thou?* soundtrack did.

'Love Is The Truth'
Jack wrote this song (also known online as 'What Goes Around Comes Around') for a Coca-Cola commercial in 2006. Jack, the aesthete, was no doubt a fan of Coke's iconic red-and-white designs, and he saw this 'as an opportunity to record an inspirational song that could reach a worldwide

audience', as per his notes on the track for the *Acoustic Recordings* compilation. The acoustic mix on that album is the only commercially available version of this song. The ad itself was aired only once and it was not available online for a long time. This is perhaps because Coke wanted to use 'We're Going To Be Friends' and Jack gave them this instead, which they didn't like. Jack's few remaining trad punk fans might not have liked him blatantly cosying up to a multinational corporation, but this is hardly Muzak. While it's not at the level of the classic 'Buy The World A Coke' jingle, it deserved to be more widely heard.

'Another Way To Die'
In 2008, Jack was tapped for one of the ultimate honours in popular music: writing an opening credits song for the latest James Bond film, Daniel Craig's second outing, *Quantum Of Solace*. Jack aimed for the slow and soulful tone of classic Bond themes like 'Goldfinger', with powerful brass bursts from The Memphis Horns, fatalistic lyrics well-suited to Craig's more down-to-earth Bond and R&B singer Alicia Keys for additional vocal power. This had the potential to be one of the best Bond themes ever.

Note that word: 'potential'. While this single hit the Top Ten in various European countries, it is generally ranked as one of the worst Bond themes. The problem is in the production. Keys added her vocals after the song was recorded, and her and Jack's voices clash horribly, which exacerbates the already abrasive tone of the song. The arrangement somehow manages to be sluggish and overly cluttered at the same time. Jack has recorded worse songs, but this may be his most disappointing self-inflicted failure.

'Fly Farm Blues'
This song was released in 2009 as a single-sided 7" and digital download. Jack wrote and recorded it in a single session, as shown in the movie *It Might Get Loud* (see 'Videos'). It's a rudimentary country blues that deliberately sounds 80 years old. As a demonstration of Jack's work ethic, it's impressive. As a song, it lacks a memorable tune or hook.

'Love Is Blindness' (Adam Clayton, Dave Evans, Paul Hewson, Larry Mullen Jr.)
This U2 cover was first released in the December 2011 edition of *Q* magazine, on the *(Ăhk-to˘ong Ba ̄y-bi) Covered* compilation, a 20th-anniversary tribute to U2's *Achtung Baby* album. It was the B-side of 'Sixteen Saltines' and is a bonus track on the Japanese edition of *Blunderbuss*. More significantly, it was included on the soundtrack of Baz Luhrmann's 2013 film adaptation of *The Great Gatsby*, which is where it reached Generation Z and has since become one of Jack's best-known solo songs.

The original was an anomaly even on U2's eclectic *Achtung Baby*, being closer to Bryan Ferry's cabaret blues than the Irish band's typical 'big music'. Jack dragged to the surface all the pain and self-loathing that Bono sublimated, and his desperate gasping and fiery guitar playing make it sound like he is trying to exorcise his failed marriage to Karen Elson.

'You Know That I Know' (Hank Williams)
This was released on the 2011 various artists album *The Lost Notebooks Of Hank Williams*. This project involved recently unearthed lyrics by country icon Hank Williams being put to music by roots rock luminaries. Alongside Jack, these included Bob Dylan, Levon Helm, Lucinda Williams and Merle Haggard. Not bad company to be in. That said, these lyrics aren't among Williams' most interesting, and Jack's music is, at best, a close approximation of classic honky-tonk. Fun, but lightweight.

'Machine Gun Silhouette'
This was the B-side of the 'Love Interruption' single and is included on *Acoustic Recordings*. The song is about competing with people at auctions. It's probably a metaphor, although for what, I could not tell you.

'Inaccessible Mystery'
This was the B-side of the 'Freedom At 21' single. It is about a 63-year-old man who is jealous of his 22-year-old lover's freedom. It is the self-deprecating flip of the A-side. It could also be a reference to Kiss' classic 'Goin' Blind', which includes the even more pronounced age gap: he's 93 and she's 16!

'Blues On Two Trees'
This was the B-side of the 'I'm Shakin'' single. It's an extended pun based on the old joke, 'Why don't you make like a tree, and leave?' Here, the trees symbolise commitment and there are lines about them 'barking'. This is not Jack's sharpest piece of writing.

'Just One Drink' (acoustic version)
This all-acoustic version of this song is available on the *Acoustic Recordings* compilation.

'Red Headed Stranger' (Edith Lindeman, Carl Stutz)
This was the title track of Willie Nelson's iconic 1975 album, that became the cornerstone of the 'outlaw country' movement. Jack recorded it as a duet with Willie in the Third Man record booth, and it was released in 2016 as a single-sided 6" (yes, that's right).

'Power Of My Love' (Bernie Baum, Bill Giant, Florence Kaye)
This was the B-Side of the 'Lazaretto' single. It is surprising that it took until 2014 for Jack to cover Elvis Presley, especially considering he once played

The King on film (see 'Videos'). Thankfully, when he finally got around to it, he went for a beloved deep cut instead of a well-worn hit. This song was recorded by Elvis for his career-best 1969 album *From Elvis In Memphis*. Jack delivers his version with appropriate 'oomph', and plays a particularly demented guitar solo. This was remixed for Baz Luhrmann's 2022 film *Elvis* as a duet between Jack and Presley, a bad idea well-executed.

'Parallel'
This was the B-side of the 'Would You Fight For My Love' vinyl single. It's a sweet country love song about a couple that think in unison.

'Blue Light, Red Light (Someone's There)' (Harry Connick Jr, Ramsey McLean)
This was the B-Side of the 'That Black Bat Licorice' single. It is a cover of a 1991 song by big band revivalist Harry Connick Jr. Connick Jr. is, in my humble opinion, an underrated songwriter, and this is a good example of his and McLean's elliptical but approachable style. It's about a down-on-his-luck guy with big dreams for him and his girlfriend. Jack's nephew Josh Gillis plays Rhodes piano, and Jack demonstrates he could make a decent jazz crooner album.

Lazaretto Hidden Tracks
There are two untitled tracks hidden under the label on either side on the Lazaretto 'Ultra edition' vinyl. Both are less than a minute long. Side A is Jack goofing on Curtis Mayfield's 'Pusher Man'. Side B is some toddlers (presumably Jack's) mumbling a nursery rhyme, and it sounds like something out of a horror movie.

'You Are The Sunshine Of My Life' (Stevie Wonder)
This strangely ominous cover of Stevie Wonder's 1972 soul classic was released as a non-album single in 2016. The A-side is a straight cover, while the B-side has backing vocals from The Muppets' house band The Electric Mayhem. One of the great rock 'n' soul revues of the 1970s, The Electric Mayhem's profile has waned since The Muppets' TV show was cancelled. Nevertheless, Jack undoubtedly had to call in a huge favour to get them on this track. Rumours about Jack dating lead guitarist Janice were apparently false, but there is evidence that Meg gave Animal some drumming lessons ...

'Matrimonial Intentions' (traditional)
'Mama's Angel Child' (Johnny Watson)
These two country blues tunes were recorded for the soundtrack to the film *The American Epic Sessions* (see 'Videos'). The first is a traditional song about tough-talking women putting commitment-phobic men in their place. The second was written by a blues artist who performed as Daddy Stovepipe and

is a classic lonesome blues lament. See 'Productions' for more information on this album.

'Battle Cry'

This riff-fest was released as a non-album, single-sided 7" for Record Store Day in 2017. There is a CD version listed on Discogs that has a variety of different edits, but the 2:32 version is the one on streaming services. There are no lyrics other than 'Hey!', thus, making this a literal battle cry.

Collaborations & Guest Appearances

These are recordings by other artists on which Jack has a prominent guest role as vocalist and/or musician, listed chronologically.

Goober & The Peas
The Jet-Age Genius Of Goober & The Peas (1995)
Jack, credited as John Gillis, played drums on this album by these Detroit cowpunks. He also appears in their video for the song 'Loose Lips'.

2-Star Tabernacle featuring Andre Williams
'Lily White Mama And Jet Black Daddy' (Andre Williams)
'Ramblin' Man' (Hank Williams)
This 1998 7" single was a collaboration between one of Jack's early bands, 2-Star Tabernacle, and R&B legend Andre Williams, co-writer of 'Shake A Tail Feather'. Jack and Williams duet on 'Lily White Mama...', which is about the tribulations of being mixed race. Subtle it ain't, but there's some tasty guitar work.

The Hank Williams cover on the B-side features Jack on piano. In 2002, both songs were made available on the Bloodshot Records compilation *Making Singles Drinking Doubles*.

The Hentchmen
'Psycho Daisies' (Jeff Beck, Chris Dreja, Jim McCarty, Jimmy Page, Keith Relf)
'Some Other Guy' (Richie Barrett, Jerry Leiber, Mike Stoller)
Jack produced and played guitar on this 1998 single by the Hentchmen. The A-side is a Yardbirds cover, while the B-side was a live staple of the pre-fame Beatles. Jack also played live with the Hentchmen occasionally and played bass on their *Hentch-Forth* album.

The Go
Whatcha Doin' (1999)
Jack played lead guitar on this debut album from The Go, and co-wrote two songs, 'Keep On Trash' and 'Time For Moon'. This album was released by the iconic Seattle label Sub Pop in 1999. It is a fine example of unpretentious party rock, and, back in the late 1990s, if one had to bet on one band from the Detroit scene making it big, it would have been The Go. But this record didn't connect, and the band changed their line-up, then their sound, then their label, and lost all momentum.

'The only band I've been fired from', Jack said, according to author Nick Hasted. But feelings weren't hurt badly enough to preclude The Go from opening for The White Stripes on their tour supporting *Elephant*. A live album from Jack's time with the band – *Live At The Gold Dollar* – was released by Third Man Records in 2016.

The Upholsters
Makers Of High Grade Suites (2000)
This EP was the only official release by The Upholsters, the band Jack formed with his mentor Brian Muldoon. There are three songs: covers of 'I Ain't Superstitious' by Willie Dixon and 'Pain (Gimme Sympathy)' by Jack Starr, plus one original, 'Apple Of My Eye' (W.E. Klomp, Brian Muldoon, Jack White). You can hear the latter on YouTube and it sounds a lot like early White Stripes with more conventional rock drumming.

Electric Six
'Danger! High Voltage' (Steve Nawara, Tyler Spencer)
This 2003 dance-punk goof by Detroit band Electric Six, from their album *Fire*, is one of the great one-hit wonders of the 2000s. It was initially recorded when Electric Six were known as The Wildbunch. Jack sang on this re-recording, with the stipulation that he didn't sing the 'Fire at the Taco Bell!' line because he didn't want to be seen as endorsing that restaurant. The funky riff and pounding beat make this an effective floor-filler, even as it parodies disco conventions. The contrast between the macho delivery of frontman Dick Valentine and Jack's hysterical shrieking gives the song its subversive edge.

Electric Six claim that Jack spun this for his new label, XL Records, because they signed the band. The song was remixed to make it radio-friendly, and it was duly a big hit. The video – which saw Jack's vocals mimed by a middle-aged woman wearing a bustier with light-up breasts – had a budget of $100,000. This was the biggest budgeted promotional push Jack had yet been involved in, which is ironic because it wasn't even clear that it was him on the record! He was credited as John S. O'Leary, and the band consistently denied it was him.

Loretta Lynn
'Portland Oregon' (Loretta Lynn)
This was the second single from Loretta Lynn's *Van Lear Rose* album (see 'Productions'). Lynn insisted on recording a duet with Jack, and this song was an interesting choice given its origins. According to an interview Lynn did with *60 Minutes* in 2005, the song was inspired by when she pretended to have had an affair with her guitarist to make her philandering husband jealous. The song was named after the city where the imaginary liaison took place, and Jack played the part of the pretend paramour.

The song is a brilliant piece of country music storytelling, and Jack's arrangement elevates it to a whole other level. It opens with squalling acid rock guitar that ebbs and flows for a full minute-and-a-half before Lynn enters with the perfect opening line: 'Well Portland Oregon and slow gin fizz, if that ain't love then tell me what is'. She and Jack trade lines before singing together at the climax. Their voices are ideally matched, not in note-perfect harmony, but in spirit.

The chemistry between the two was palpable when they performed the song together on the *Late Show With David Letterman*. The music video took things up a notch, with Jack and Lynn making bedroom eyes at each other in a club.

This song won Lynn and Jack the Grammy Award for Best Country Collaboration with Vocals, and rightly so. In my opinion, this is one of the top five songs Jack has ever been involved in.

Beck
'Go It Alone' (Beck Hansen, John King, Michael Simpson, Jack White)
'I Just Started Hating Some People Today' (Beck Hansen)
'Blue Randy' (Beck Hansen)
Californian singer-songwriter Beck Hansen is like a mirror image of Jack in many ways. They both started out putting their own warped spin on roots music – lo-fi 'anti-folk' in Beck's case – but while Jack gradually moved away from pastiche, Beck leaned into it.

Beck's postmodern, sample-heavy, hip-hop-adjacent alt-pop is very distinct from Jack's 'keep it real' ethos. But both artists have a determined work ethic, a healthy disdain for contemporary tend-chasing and a willingness to collaborate.

The first song listed is an album track from Beck's 2005 album *Guero*, on which Jack plays bass. The other two are the A and B-side of a 2012 single Beck recorded especially for Third Man Records. Jack plays drums and guitar, and contributes 'punk vocals'.

Danger Mouse and Daniele Luppi
'The Rose With The Broken Neck' (Brian Burton, Daniele Luppi, Jack White)
'Two Against One' (Brian Burton, Daniele Luppi, Jack White)
'The World' (Brian Burton, Daniele Luppi, Jack White)
These three songs are from the 2011 album *Rome*, a collaboration between American producer Danger Mouse (né: Brian Burton) and Italian composer Daniele Luppi. It is a tribute to the soundtrack work of Ennio Morricone, featuring the original choir from the *The Good, The Bad And The Ugly* score, and was recorded using (of course) vintage equipment. Jack recorded vocals for these three songs and they're all worth hearing, with the dramatic 'Two Against One' being the pick of the pack. Jack recorded each track using different vocal ranges – bass, alto and tenor – and Burton mixed the takes together.

It is interesting that Jack collaborated with Danger Mouse, given his antipathy towards The Black Keys, who in 2011, were in the middle of a golden run of albums produced by Burton. There were reports that Jack picked a fight with The Black Keys' Patrick Carney in New York, but the pair have since reconciled.

Beyoncé
'Don't Hurt Yourself' (Diana Gordon, Beyoncé Knowles, Jack White, John Bonham, John Paul Jones, Robert Plant, Jimmy Page)
Jack co-produced, plays bass and sings the title hook on this song from Beyoncé's 2016 album *Lemonade*. If you're wondering about those writing credits, it's because the song uses a drum sample from Led Zeppelin's 'When The Levee Breaks'.

Pop-phobics might scoff, but this is a near-perfect blend of rock and modern R&B. Jack's production gives the music a nervy, pressure-cooker feel, and Beyoncé attacks the lyrics hard. Jack said to NPR: 'She took just sort of a sketch of a lyrical outline and turned it into the most bodacious, vicious, incredible song. I don't even know what you'd classify it as – soul, rock and roll, whatever'. I'd say it's as close as it gets these days to the mid-1970s Tina Turner sound.

It is possible that Jack has earned more royalties from this one song than from the rest of his solo work combined. It is the first song listed on his Apple Music page, after all. That's not entirely surprising, given that Beyoncé is, by any measure, one of the most popular and acclaimed pop stars in the world. This is less a case of her seeking approval from a rock audience, and more like her giving a struggling indie musician a leg-up. It is also a sign of how times have changed and old genre distinctions no longer matter.

A Tribe Called Quest
'Solid Wall Of Sound' (Kamaal Fareed, Malik Taylor, Jack White)
'Ego' (Kamaal Fareed, Jack White)
'The Donald' (Kamaal Fareed)
Jack contributes guitar to these three songs, and vocals to the first, from the 2016 album *We Got It From Here... Thank You 4 Your Service* by hip-hop group A Tribe Called Quest. This was the Tribe's first album since 1998, and it's likely their last due to the death of member Phife Dawg (né: Malik Taylor) from diabetes ('The Donald' is a tribute to him). 'Solid Wall Of Sound' is based on a sample of 'Bennie And The Jets' by Elton John, whom Jack would also collaborate with (see below). 'Ego' includes a sample of György Ligeti's music used in *2001: A Space Odyssey*! All three songs are worth hearing, but for an example of A Tribe Called Quest in their absolute prime, check out their 1991 album *The Low-End Theory*. Jack later co-wrote 'Hi-De-Ho' with member Q-Tip (né: Kamall Fareed).

Elton John
'2 Fingers Of Whiskey' (Elton John, Bernie Taupin)
Jack duets with Elton John on this song from the American Epic Sessions project (see 'Productions'). Featuring on a brand new John/Taupin song is certainly an honour, and Jack brings his A-game to this boogie-woogie throwback.

Tyler, The Creator
'Are We Still Friends?' (Tyler Okonma, Al Green)

Jack plays guitar on this track from controversial rapper Tyler, The Creator's 2019 *Igor* album. He went uncredited because, according to Tyler, he could not hear his contributions.

Compilations

There are two official Jack White compilations currently available:

Acoustic Recordings 1998–2016

If any artist deserves a sprawling multiple-disc compilation covering all his various bands, mixing hits, fan favourites, rarities, and unreleased songs – in the vein of Neil Young's awesome *Decade* – it is Jack White. Until Jack feels like compiling that, this 2016 collection is the best we have. It is a themed compilation, focusing on his acoustic-based songs, with cuts from The White Stripes, The Raconteurs and his solo work. Sequenced chronologically, it demonstrates one facet of Jack's musical maturation. It is not a good introduction for newbies, but it has value as a vinyl collectable for hardcore fans.

Rarities include 'Never Far Away' from the *Cold Mountain* soundtrack; the acoustic versions of 'Top Yourself', 'Carolina Drama', 'Machine Gun Silhouette' and 'Just One Drink'; beefed-up mixes of 'Apple Blossom', 'I'm Bound To Pack It Up', 'Hip (Eponymous) Poor Boy' and 'I Guess I Should Go To Sleep'; and the B-side 'Honey, We Can't Afford To Look This Cheap'. The otherwise unavailable songs are 'City Lights' and 'Love Is The Truth'.

The White Stripes Greatest Hits

This was released in 2020 on double-vinyl and digitally – it is too long for a CD edition. A White Stripes compilation released just after *Icky Thump* – or even after they officially dissolved in 2011 – would likely have sold well and remained a valuable catalogue item. Released when it was, this was more of a symbolic gesture. As Jack said in the press release: 'We get that the idea of 'Greatest Hits' may seem irrelevant in the era of streaming, but we also wholeheartedly believe that great bands deserve a 'Greatest Hits'.

He's not wrong, as there are many great artists who are better known for their hits compilations than they are for their long-players: ABBA, Bob Marley, Madonna, Tom Petty. Whereas those collections are neat and easily digestible, this is a sprawling 26-song collection sequenced non-chronologically that saves many of the band's biggest hits for the back half. The choice of songs is idiosyncratic: there's 'Screwdriver', 'The Nurse' and 'I Fought Piranhas', but no 'There's No Home For You Here' or 'You Don't Know What Love Is'. Fortunately, 'Ball And Biscuit' is included. There are two rarities as well: 'Let's Shake Hands' and the studio version of 'Jolene'. While these are all undeniably great songs, a tighter and tidier single LP collection would pack more punch.

Live Recordings

From The White Stripes' debut on, Jack's live performances have been well documented, and since he started Third Man Records, he's been releasing archival recordings from all stages of his career. Between those, the various live recordings scattered across B-sides and a thriving bootleg market, if you want to find a live performance of your favourite Jack White song, you shouldn't have to look too far.

There are a handful of 'canonical' live recordings that should be singled out for special attention, listed here in order of recording. Every album, other than *Under Great White Northern Lights*, was released as part of the Third Man Records Vault series. These and many more shows are legally available for streaming or purchase on the website nugs.net.

Live At The Gold Dollar

This is a recording of The White Stripes' first live appearance on 14 August 1997. The sound is terrific compared to most other early live recordings from bands.

Live On The Garden Bowl Lanes July 9, 1999

Credited to Jack White And The Bricks, this gives you a chance to hear pre-White Stripes versions of songs such as 'Dead Leaves And The Dirty Ground', recorded with a four-piece band that includes Brendan Benson on guitar.

Peel Sessions

The White Stripes recorded these at John Peel's country house in 2001 for broadcast on his BBC Radio 1 show. The sound quality is not perfect, but every song is played with 150% speed and energy. There are a handful of otherwise unavailable covers, but on the whole, this is most interesting as a historical document of the last great indie rock band John Peel had a hand in breaking before he died in 2004. As revealed in the 2005 documentary *John Peel's Record Box*, his box of 130 favourite singles included 11 by The White Stripes, more than any other artist.

Under Amazonian Lights

From The White Stripes' *Get Behind Me Satan* tour in 2005, recorded on the day Jack married Karen Elson.

Under Great White Northern Lights

This was recorded on The White Stripes' 2007 tour through Canada, and released in 2010 by V2 Records to accompany the documentary of the same name (see 'Videos'). This served as a surprise epitaph for the band, and as such, it is fondly regarded by many fans. It is impeccably recorded and includes many of their best songs, so if you fancy a taster of The White Stripes live, this compilation is a nifty one-stop shop. There is also a companion album, *B-Shows*, available from Third Man.

Live In Mississippi
This is a recording of the last ever White Stripes concert on 31 July 2007.

Live At The Mayen, Los Angeles
There are shockingly few Dead Weather live albums out there, relative to Jack's other projects. This show from 2009 is worth tracking down as it mixes album tracks and covers, and includes a Blu-ray of the show.

Live At Third Man Records
Jack's first solo live album, also from 2012, documents his performances with alternate support bands, the all-male Peacocks and the all-female Buzzards.

Live In Tulsa
Of all the available live Raconteurs recordings, this three-LP compilation from various October 2019 concerts is the most exhaustive and comes with a Blu-ray of acoustic performances from Jack and Benson.

The Supply Chain Issues Tour: Detroit, Masonic Temple, April 8 2022
During this solo concert, Jack proposed to guitarist Olivia Jean during 'Hotel Yorba', and married her live on stage before continuing the show! The whole concert is worth hearing, although the setlist was necessarily abbreviated!

Productions

Jack has been producing music for almost as long as he's been a professional musician. He is not the kind of producer who leaves a distinctive sonic thumbprint on other artists, like Daniel Lanois or Mutt Lange. His work is more in the vein of undersung yeomen of the 1970s, such as Tom Dowd and Glyn Johns. Jack is all about assembling the right crew and facilitating the right environment for the artist to realise the best version of their sound.

This is not an exhaustive overview of his behind-the-boards work, merely a selection of his best and most notable, in order of release.

Soledad Brothers – Soledad Brothers (2000)

Jack recorded the self-titled debut album from these fellow Detroiters, while Meg played percussion. Jack also appears on their non-album song 'Johnny's Death Letter', apparently playing a snow shovel!

Various Artists – The Sympathetic Sounds Of Detroit (2001)

Jack curated this compilation for the Sympathy For The Record Industry label, recording all the artists' contributions in his attic. The Hentchmen's Tim Purrier said to author Nick Hasted: 'We just went over the Jack's house and watched TV for a little bit. Went up and plugged into his amps and recorded a song of ours he liked on his gear'. The liner notes are worth reading, as Jack proves a poor prophet: 'No suit from LA or New York is going to fly to Detroit to check out a band and hand out business cards'.

The Von Bondies – Lack Of Communication (2001)

Jack produced the debut by these Detroit garage rockers while he was dating their guitarist Marcie Bolen. He was an early champion of the band and invited them to support The White Stripes for their European tour in 2001. However, after this album's release, singer Jason Stollsteimer began badmouthing Jack's production work. On 13 December 2003, Jack was charged with assaulting Stollsteimer. Jack claims he was provoked but nevertheless, pled guilty to a misdemeanour assault on 9 March 2004. This was the first major press scandal of Jack's career. It contributed to his reputation as a volatile weirdo but didn't harm his career in the long run. The incident brought attention to The Von Bondies, but their 2004 follow-up album, *Pawn Shoppe Heart*, didn't deliver and the band faded away.

Loretta Lynn – Van Lear Rose (2004)

This album deserves extra attention as it is the most critically acclaimed of Jack's production jobs. I would go so far as to say it's one of the top five albums he's been a part of.

Lynn was initially hesitant when Jack offered to produce a new album for her. She did not want this Midwestern rocker to turn a feisty Southern dame into a pop novelty act. But Jack was not about to follow current trends for how to 'reinvent' a classic artist. By 2003, the 'Boomer icon comeback record' had become something of a cliché unto itself. They generally came in two forms. There was the star-studded celebration, where peers and supplicants collaborated on new versions of old classics. See Frank Sinatra's *Duets*, Ray Charles' *Genius Loves Company* and Jerry Lee Lewis' *Last Man Standing*. These can come across as cynical because if you corral enough big names for the project, you're bound to shift units, even if the product is middling. The other approach was pioneered by superproducer Rick Rubin on his *American* series for Johnny Cash: stripped-down, sombre and dignified, and an eclectic selection of covers to bait the hipsters. This worked for Cash and Neil Diamond, and it later would for Tom Jones.

Jack had something else in mind. He had been a Loretta Lynn fan ever since he saw the biopic *Coal Miner's Daughter* as a child. That movie began his fascination with the South, which was piqued again by filming *Cold Mountain*. In *Mojo* in 2002, he called Lynn 'the greatest female singer-songwriter of the 20th Century'. Part of why he liked her was that 'She was not a fake product of the Nashville system'. So he didn't want her to sound like other artists. He decided to play into Lynn's honest and ornery persona.

After years of singing other people's songs, Lynn had literal grocery bags filled with lyrics, so this album would be almost entirely self-composed. This was not a Jack White album featuring Loretta Lynn; the county legend was the star. Not that the music was a secondary consideration. Jack assembled a crack band: bassist Jack Lawrence and drummer Patrick Keeler from The Greenhornes, plus Dave Feeny on slide guitar, pedal steel and dobro. With Jack also on guitar, they recorded the album in 12 days. They would pick a set of lyrics, work up a song around it and record it in 20 minutes. Jack treated every song as the A-side of its own 45, to avoid thinking of the album as one blur of undifferentiated sound. One highlight, the raucous 'Have Mercy', was written for Elvis, although the bolero rhythm more resembles Roy Orbison's 'Running Scared'. Jack gave a lovely performance of the title track at a Country Music Television tribute to Lynn after her death in 2022.

Van Lear Rose went to number 24 on the *Billboard* 200, went to number two on the country charts and won the Grammy for Best Country Album. For a 72-year-old country musician, it was an incredible achievement, especially considering that the album had zero support from corporate country radio. But, like The White Stripes' Dolly Parton cover, this album helped convince indie kids to give authentic country music a proper listen.

Keren Elson – The Ghost Who Walks (2010)
Jack decided to produce an album for his then-wife after hearing her sing original songs around their home. He also played drums, and Jack Lawrence and Dean Fertita also contributed. The title was a schoolyard nickname for her (and not a reference to The Phantom).

Remember in *Citizen Kane* when Kane builds an opera house for his wife to perform in even though she can't sing? This is not like that. Elson has a pleasantly tough voice and wrote solid songs. This album is well worth checking out if you're a fan of Amy Winehouse's retro-soul sound.

Elson also released *Live At Third Man Records* in 2012, and two albums on other labels. But she has not worked with Jack since their *Blunderbuss* in 2012. Despite the turbulent fallout of their marriage, Elson retained enough goodwill to issue a statement defending Meg during the 2023 online brouhaha over her drumming skills.

Wanda Jackson – The Party Ain't Over (2011)

Wanda Jackson was the original Queen of Rockabilly, thanks to 1950s hits such as 'Fujiyama Mama' and 'Let's Have A Party'. She also recorded country and gospel music, making her the ideal subject for another Jack White reclamation project ala *Van Lear Rose*. But this album is a less ambitious project of more modest pleasures. Jack did not play on the album (although Keeler and Lawrence did). There are no original songs, only covers. Some of these were disappointingly predictable choices ('Shakin' All Over', 'Rip It Up'), but there were a couple of curveballs. Amy Winehouse's 'You Know I'm No Good' already sounds like a decades-old standard, and Jackson turns Bob Dylan's 'Thunder On the Mountain' into a retro rave-up. Her voice is, let's say, 'well-weathered'. But if you adjust your expectations, you'll find this is a fun listen. Jackson also released *Live At Third Man Records* in 2011.

Neil Young – A Letter Home (2014)

Jack co-produced this covers collection with Young, and it was recorded entirely using the Third Man Records refurbished 1947 Voice-o-Graph vinyl recording booth. Jack plays piano and sings on the version of Willie Nelson's 'On The Road Again', and plays guitar and sings on the version of The Everly Brothers' 'I Wonder If I Care As Much'. He and Young appeared together on *The Tonight Show Starring Jimmy Fallon* with the booth and recorded Willie Nelson's 'Crazy' live on air to demonstrate the system.

Various Artists – Music From The American Epic Sessions (2017)

This collection (not to be confused with various other *American Epic* compilations tied to the same project) was co-produced by Jack and T Bone Burnett. It is a tribute to the Western Electric direct-to-disc recording system from 1925. They invited artists from across the musical spectrum to record using the device. Most recorded classic folk and blues tunes, but there are a handful of original songs, including Jack's duet with Elton John (see 'Collaborations & Guest Appearances').

If you want a handy sampler of who's who in the modern roots music scene, this will do you.

Third Man Records

Jack produced every one of the Third Man Records 'Blue Series' of limited edition 7" vinyl singles from 2009 to 2012. He rang musicians who were passing through Nashville and arranged for them to record with impromptu bands of session players. He produced tracks for a wide variety of artists, from venerable icons like Tom Jones and Elvira (yes, the TV horror hostess), to modern masters like Laura Marling and Seasick Steve, to cult artists like The Black Belles, whose singer-guitarist Olivia Jean he married in 2022.

One of the Blue Series is Jack's all-time oddest production. It's a recording of Mozart's 1782 composition 'Leck Mich Im Arsch' (this translates as 'Lick me in the arse), with lyrical additions from Detroit horror-rappers Insane Clown Posse. ICP might seem like unusual collaborators for Jack, what with their 'evil clown' make-up, absurd lyrics (e.g. 'Fuckin magnets, how do they work?' from 'Miracles') and annual trash culture festival The Gathering Of The Juggalos. But like Jack, they have maintained a decades-long music career outside of the mainstream due to their personal connection with fans. Maybe Jack should take a leaf out of their book and organise a 'Jack Fest' someday.

Videos

This is a list of Jack White-related videos, with concerts and music documentaries grouped first, followed by other projects. I am only including material that is widely available through mainstream media outlets, so no bootlegs. There are also various live films released as part of rare Third Man Records Vault packages.

Detroit Rawk!!! (2001)
This documentary, produced by the Dutch TV station VPRO, can be viewed on YouTube. It covers the emerging Detroit scene and includes priceless early footage of Jack and Meg, plus many other local musicians. Mick Collins from The Dirtbombs gives some especially interesting insights into the economic forces that shaped Detroit's entertainment scene.

Candy Coloured Blues (2003)
This unauthorised White Stripes documentary is widely available, but be warned! It contains no actual White Stripes music and very little footage of Jack and Meg. But it does include interviews with various Detroit associates and provides some context for their hometown scene.

Under Blackpool Lights (2004)
This is the first, and some would say best, White Stripes concert film, recorded at the Empress Ballroom in Blackpool, England. Among a thorough selection of early White Stripes classics, there are many covers, including the famous version of 'Jolene' that was released as a single.

It Might Get Loud (2012)
This documentary film by Davis Guggenheim talks about three notable guitarists – Jimmy Page, The Edge and Jack White – about their musical backgrounds, inspirations and techniques. Jack enthuses about his favourite song (Son House's 'Grinnin' In Your Face'), records a new song, 'Fly Farm Blues' (see 'Non-Album Tracks, B-Sides And Rarities'), and he builds a one-string guitar from junk on camera. The movie culminates in a summit where the three jam together on covers of Blind Willie Johnson's 'In My Time Of Dying' and The Band's 'The Weight'.

Something interesting about the reception of this documentary was that one might have assumed that Jack, being the new kid on the block, would cop the most pushback, as if the film was trying to elevate him to 'legend' status before he had earned it. But, in fact, it was the inclusion of The Edge that riled people the most.

Page's and White's playing is rooted in the blues, whereas The Edge credits his success to his use of effects pedals. But the film ably demonstrates that inspiration and creativity can come in many forms, and there is no single 'right way' to make great music.

Under Great White Northern Lights (2009)

This film documents The White Stripes' summer 2007 effort to perform in every province of Canada. They play various surprise gigs – including a single-note before a packed crowd. Along the way, there is some great live footage, assorted musings from Jack and much arty black-and-white footage. The final scene, where Jack reduces Meg to tears with his solo performance of 'White Moon', seems, in retrospect, like the perfect ending for The White Stripes.

Live At Montreux (2012)

This 2008 Raconteurs concert was filmed in the Swiss town of 'Smoke On The Water' fame and is part of a series of archival 'Live At Montreux' concerts. It includes performances of all the best songs from the band's first two albums.

Live From Bonnaroo (2014)
Acoustic Tour (2015)

These two Jack White solo concert films are available as part of separate LP+DVD live packages from Third Man.

The American Epic Sessions (2017)

Jack appears in this documentary about the restoration of the first electrical sound recording system from 1925. See 'Productions' for more details.

The Rosary Murders (1987)

Look fast to catch pre-teen Jack as an extra in this religious-based thriller that was partly filmed in the Holy Redeemer church, where he was an altar boy.

Cold Mountain (2003)

Jack's first acting role was in his Civil War epic directed by Anthony Minghella. His role as a travelling minstrel is substantial, and he sings a few songs (see 'Non-Album Tracks, B-Sides And Rarities').

Coffee And Cigarettes (2003)

This film by Jim Jarmusch consists of 11 short sequences with different characters chatting over the titular relaxants. Jack and Meg play 'themselves' (as siblings). Jack pontificates about outsider inventor Nikola Tesla and shows Meg a Tesla coil that he built. She is nonplussed. This is a fun sequence, but not really worth watching this whole film for.

The White Stripes met indie cinema icon Jarmusch after they played a free gig in New York in 2002. He remained a fan of theirs and gave Jack a shout-out in his 2014 film *Only Lovers Left Alive*, when vampire rock star Tom Hiddleston points out Jack's old house to lover Tilda Swinton.

Walk Hard: The Dewey Cox Story (2007)

This spoof movie directed by Jake Kasdan is to music biopics what *Blazing Saddles* is to Westerns: a brutally precise and hilarious skewering that exposes the clichés of the genre. It is loosely based on the Johnny Cash biopic *Walk The Line* but draws from the rock 'n' roll lore of Elvis Presley, The Beatles, Bob Dylan and The Beach Boys. Jack appears in one scene as Elvis, mumbling bizarre improvised gibberish about his karate skills. It's funnier than it sounds, honest.

The Killers Of The Flower Moon (2023)

Jack has a small role in this movie directed by Martin Scorsese, based on the book of the same name by David Grann, about a series of murders in the 1920s in the Native American Osage community. Jack plays an actor in a radio dramatisation – just about the perfect role for this lover of outdated media. Scorsese is famous for his adroit use of classic rock songs in his movies, and he obviously still has a good ear, as alongside Jack, the cast includes other modern Americana luminaries, Jason Isbell and Sturgill Simpson.

The Best Of Jack White

Just for fun, I've ranked every Jack White album and compiled a list of his Top 20 songs. I tried to balance my personal taste with critical acclaim, fan favouritism and cultural impact. I doubt every fan will agree – that's to be expected with a catalogue as diverse and sometimes divisive as Jack's. I went through multiple drafts of these lists, and I'm still not entirely satisfied with my rankings! So consider these merely suggestions for new fans.

All Albums Ranked

1. *Elephant*
2. *White Blood Cells*
3. *Broken Boy Soldiers*
4. *Lazaretto*
5. *Blunderbuss*
6. *De Stijl*
7. *Get Behind Me Satan*
8. *Icky Thump*
9. *Consolers Of The Lonely*
10. *Horehound*
11. *Fear Of The Dawn*
12. *Dodge And Burn*
13. *Help Us Stranger*
14. *The White Stripes*
15. *Entering Heaven Alive*
16. *Sea Of Cowards*
17. *Boarding House Reach*

Top 20 Songs

1. 'Ball And Biscuit'
2. 'Seven Nation Army'
3. 'Fell In Love With A Girl'
4. 'We're Going To Be Friends'
5. 'Icky Thump'
6. 'Steady, As She Goes'
7. 'My Doorbell'
8. 'Hotel Yorba'
9. 'Dead Leaves And The Dirty Ground'
10. 'Carolina Drama'
11. 'Blue Veins'
12. 'Treat Me Like Your Mother'
13. 'Old Enough'
14. 'Hands'
15. 'Lazaretto'
16. 'Freedom At 21'

17. 'The Hardest Button To Button'
18. 'The Denial Twist'
19. 'Hello Operator'
20. 'Love Interruption'

Bibliography

ALT 98.7., 'Jack White Talks "Boarding House Reach", Chris Rock, Black Mirror, Third Man Records & More!' (YouTube, 20 March 2018)

Boilen, B., 'Jack White's 'Lazaretto': The All Songs interview' (*NPR.com*, 20 May 2014)

Bosso, J. 'Jack White on The White Stripes' future' (*Musicradar.com*, 6 May 2009)

Bovey, S., *Five Years Ahead Of My Time: Garage Rock From The 1950s To The Present* (Reaktion Books, 2019)

Cameron, K., 'The Sweetheart Deal' (*The Guardian*, 29 March 2003)

Cameron, K., 'Gang of four' (*Mojo*, May 2006)

Chick, S., 'Heart of Darkness' (*Mojo*, August 2005)

Chick, S., 'How to buy: Jack White' (*Mojo*, December 2015)

Cross, A., 'A conversation with Jack White about music, the universe and everything' (*Global News*, 25 March 2018)

Currin, G. H., 'All my colours (*Mojo*, May 2022)

Goodman, L., *Meet Me In The Bathroom: Rebirth and Rock and Roll in New York City 2001-2011* (Dey St., 2017)

Handyside, C., *Fell In Love With A Band: The Story of The White Stripes* (St. Martin's Press, 2004)

Hasted, N., *Jack White: How He Built An Empire From The Blues* (Omnibus Press, 2016)

Hodgkinson, W., 'I don't want to give in to the digital age' (*The Guardian*, 3 July 2009)

Hodgkinson, W., 'Little boy blue' (*Mojo*, August 2014)

Hoskyns, IB, 'Jack White interview' (*Uncut*, November 2009)

Hyden, S., *Twilight Of The Gods: A Journey To The End Of Classic Rock* (Dey St., 2019)

Ivie, D., 'Jack White on the most stubborn and prophetic music of his career' (*Vulture.com*, 21 July 2022)

Male, A., 'Basic instinct' (*Mojo*, September 2002)

Male, A., 'Jack White: The Mojo interview' (*Mojo*, July 2007)

Male, A., 'The history man' (*Mojo*, November 2018)

Marcus, G., *Invisible Republic* (Picador, 1997)

McBain, H. (Ed.), NME Icons: Jack White (*IPC Media*, 2011)

McCollum, B., 'Detroit's 100 Greatest Songs' (*Detroit Free Press*, 5 June 2016)

Mulvey, I., 'The same boy you've always known?' (*Uncut*, May 2012)

Needham, A., 'Review: The White Stripes – Get Behind Me Satan' (*NME*, 12 September 2005)

Nicolson, B., 'White out' (*NME*, 12 February 2011)

NP Staff, 'Jack White On Detroit, Beyoncé and where songs come from' (*NPR. com*, 10 September 2016)

Robinson, J. (Ed.), *The White Stripes: The Ultimate Music Guide* (*NME* Networks, 2023)

Rolling Stone.com, 'Jack White Reveals Everything You Need to Know About 'Lazaretto'' (*Rolling Stone*, 22 May 2014)

Rotondi, J. V., '"Fear of the Dawn" is the best guitar playing that I've ever done': Jack White on his incendiary solo album', (*Guitar Player*, 11 June 2022)

Simpson, D., 'Jack White on the Mississippi blues artists: "They changed the world"' (*The Guardian*, 8 March 2013)

Weiner, J., 'Jack White: The Strange World of a Rock & Roll Willy Wonka' (*Rolling Stone*, 21 May 2014)

White, J., 'Iggy Pop interview' (*Mojo*, October 2003)

On Track series
Allman Brothers Band – Andrew Wild 978-1-78952-252-5
Tori Amos – Lisa Torem 978-1-78952-142-9
Aphex Twin – Beau Waddell 978-1-78952-267-9
Asia – Peter Braidis 978-1-78952-099-6
Badfinger – Robert Day-Webb 978-1-878952-176-4
Barclay James Harvest – Keith and Monica Domone 978-1-78952-067-5
Beck – Arthur Lizie 978-1-78952-258-7
The Beatles – Andrew Wild 978-1-78952-009-5
The Beatles Solo 1969-1980 – Andrew Wild 978-1-78952-030-9
Blue Oyster Cult – Jacob Holm-Lupo 978-1-78952-007-1
Blur – Matt Bishop 978-178952-164-1
Marc Bolan and T.Rex – Peter Gallagher 978-1-78952-124-5
Kate Bush – Bill Thomas 978-1-78952-097-2
Camel – Hamish Kuzminski 978-1-78952-040-8
Captain Beefheart – Opher Goodwin 978-1-78952-235-8
Caravan – Andy Boot 978-1-78952-127-6
Cardiacs – Eric Benac 978-1-78952-131-3
Nick Cave and The Bad Seeds – Dominic Sanderson 978-1-78952-240-2
Eric Clapton Solo – Andrew Wild 978-1-78952-141-2
The Clash – Nick Assirati 978-1-78952-077-4
Elvis Costello and The Attractions – Georg Purvis 978-1-78952-129-0
Crosby, Stills and Nash – Andrew Wild 978-1-78952-039-2
Creedence Clearwater Revival – Tony Thompson 978-178952-237-2
The Damned – Morgan Brown 978-1-78952-136-8
Deep Purple and Rainbow 1968-79 – Steve Pilkington 978-1-78952-002-6
Dire Straits – Andrew Wild 978-1-78952-044-6
The Doors – Tony Thompson 978-1-78952-137-5
Dream Theater – Jordan Blum 978-1-78952-050-7
Eagles – John Van der Kiste 978-1-78952-260-0
Earth, Wind and Fire – Bud Wilkins 978-1-78952-272-3
Electric Light Orchestra – Barry Delve 978-1-78952-152-8
Emerson Lake and Palmer – Mike Goode 978-1-78952-000-2
Fairport Convention – Kevan Furbank 978-1-78952-051-4
Peter Gabriel – Graeme Scarfe 978-1-78952-138-2
Genesis – Stuart MacFarlane 978-1-78952-005-7
Gentle Giant – Gary Steel 978-1-78952-058-3
Gong – Kevan Furbank 978-1-78952-082-8
Green Day – William E. Spevack 978-1-78952-261-7
Hall and Oates – Ian Abrahams 978-1-78952-167-2
Hawkwind – Duncan Harris 978-1-78952-052-1
Peter Hammill – Richard Rees Jones 978-1-78952-163-4
Roy Harper – Opher Goodwin 978-1-78952-130-6

Jimi Hendrix – Emma Stott 978-1-78952-175-7
The Hollies – Andrew Darlington 978-1-78952-159-7
Horslips – Richard James 978-1-78952-263-1
The Human League and The Sheffield Scene –
Andrew Darlington 978-1-78952-186-3
The Incredible String Band – Tim Moon 978-1-78952-107-8
Iron Maiden – Steve Pilkington 978-1-78952-061-3
Joe Jackson – Richard James 978-1-78952-189-4
Jefferson Airplane – Richard Butterworth 978-1-78952-143-6
Jethro Tull – Jordan Blum 978-1-78952-016-3
Elton John in the 1970s – Peter Kearns 978-1-78952-034-7
Billy Joel – Lisa Torem 978-1-78952-183-2
Judas Priest – John Tucker 978-1-78952-018-7
Kansas – Kevin Cummings 978-1-78952-057-6
The Kinks – Martin Hutchinson 978-1-78952-172-6
Korn – Matt Karpe 978-1-78952-153-5
Led Zeppelin – Steve Pilkington 978-1-78952-151-1
Level 42 – Matt Philips 978-1-78952-102-3
Little Feat – Georg Purvis - 978-1-78952-168-9
Aimee Mann – Jez Rowden 978-1-78952-036-1
Joni Mitchell – Peter Kearns 978-1-78952-081-1
The Moody Blues – Geoffrey Feakes 978-1-78952-042-2
Motorhead – Duncan Harris 978-1-78952-173-3
Nektar – Scott Meze – 978-1-78952-257-0
New Order – Dennis Remmer – 978-1-78952-249-5
Nightwish – Simon McMurdo – 978-1-78952-270-9
Laura Nyro – Philip Ward 978-1-78952-182-5
Mike Oldfield – Ryan Yard 978-1-78952-060-6
Opeth – Jordan Blum 978-1-78-952-166-5
Pearl Jam – Ben L. Connor 978-1-78952-188-7
Tom Petty – Richard James 978-1-78952-128-3
Pink Floyd – Richard Butterworth 978-1-78952-242-6
The Police – Pete Braidis 978-1-78952-158-0
Porcupine Tree – Nick Holmes 978-1-78952-144-3
Queen – Andrew Wild 978-1-78952-003-3
Radiohead – William Allen 978-1-78952-149-8
Rancid – Paul Matts 989-1-78952-187-0
Renaissance – David Detmer 978-1-78952-062-0
REO Speedwagon – Jim Romag 978-1-78952-262-4
The Rolling Stones 1963-80 – Steve Pilkington 978-1-78952-017-0
The Smiths and Morrissey – Tommy Gunnarsson 978-1-78952-140-5
Spirit – Rev. Keith A. Gordon – 978-1-78952- 248-8
Stackridge – Alan Draper 978-1-78952-232-7

Status Quo the Frantic Four Years – Richard James 978-1-78952-160-3
Steely Dan – Jez Rowden 978-1-78952-043-9
Steve Hackett – Geoffrey Feakes 978-1-78952-098-9
Tears For Fears – Paul Clark - 978-178952-238-9
Thin Lizzy – Graeme Stroud 978-1-78952-064-4
Tool – Matt Karpe 978-1-78952-234-1
Toto – Jacob Holm-Lupo 978-1-78952-019-4
U2 – Eoghan Lyng 978-1-78952-078-1
UFO – Richard James 978-1-78952-073-6
Van Der Graaf Generator – Dan Coffey 978-1-78952-031-6
Van Halen – Morgan Brown – 9781-78952-256-3
The Who – Geoffrey Feakes 978-1-78952-076-7
Roy Wood and the Move – James R Turner 978-1-78952-008-8
Yes – Stephen Lambe 978-1-78952-001-9
Frank Zappa 1966 to 1979 – Eric Benac 978-1-78952-033-0
Warren Zevon – Peter Gallagher 978-1-78952-170-2
10CC – Peter Kearns 978-1-78952-054-5

Decades Series

The Bee Gees in the 1960s – Andrew Mon Hughes et al 978-1-78952-148-1
The Bee Gees in the 1970s – Andrew Mon Hughes et al 978-1-78952-179-5
Black Sabbath in the 1970s – Chris Sutton 978-1-78952-171-9
Britpop – Peter Richard Adams and Matt Pooler 978-1-78952-169-6
Phil Collins in the 1980s – Andrew Wild 978-1-78952-185-6
Alice Cooper in the 1970s – Chris Sutton 978-1-78952-104-7
Alice Cooper in the 1980s – Chris Sutton 978-1-78952-259-4
Curved Air in the 1970s – Laura Shenton 978-1-78952-069-9
Donovan in the 1960s – Jeff Fitzgerald 978-1-78952-233-4
Bob Dylan in the 1980s – Don Klees 978-1-78952-157-3
Brian Eno in the 1970s – Gary Parsons 978-1-78952-239-6
Faith No More in the 1990s – Matt Karpe 978-1-78952-250-1
Fleetwood Mac in the 1970s – Andrew Wild 978-1-78952-105-4
Fleetwood Mac in the 1980s – Don Klees 978-178952-254-9
Focus in the 1970s – Stephen Lambe 978-1-78952-079-8
Free and Bad Company in the 1970s – John Van der Kiste 978-1-78952-178-8
Genesis in the 1970s – Bill Thomas 978178952-146-7
George Harrison in the 1970s – Eoghan Lyng 978-1-78952-174-0
Kiss in the 1970s – Peter Gallagher 978-1-78952-246-4
Manfred Mann's Earth Band in the 1970s – John Van der Kiste 978178952-243-3
Marillion in the 1980s – Nathaniel Webb 978-1-78952-065-1
Van Morrison in the 1970s – Peter Childs - 978-1-78952-241-9
Mott the Hoople and Ian Hunter in the 1970s –
John Van der Kiste 978-1-78-952-162-7

Pink Floyd In The 1970s – Georg Purvis 978-1-78952-072-9
Suzi Quatro in the 1970s – Darren Johnson 978-1-78952-236-5
Queen in the 1970s – James Griffiths 978-1-78952-265-5
Roxy Music in the 1970s – Dave Thompson 978-1-78952-180-1
Slade in the 1970s – Darren Johnson 978-1-78952-268-6
Status Quo in the 1980s – Greg Harper 978-1-78952-244-0
Tangerine Dream in the 1970s – Stephen Palmer 978-1-78952-161-0
The Sweet in the 1970s – Darren Johnson 978-1-78952-139-9
Uriah Heep in the 1970s – Steve Pilkington 978-1-78952-103-0
Van der Graaf Generator in the 1970s – Steve Pilkington 978-1-78952-245-7
Rick Wakeman in the 1970s – Geoffrey Feakes 978-1-78952-264-8
Yes in the 1980s – Stephen Lambe with David Watkinson 978-1-78952-125-2

On Screen series
Carry On... – Stephen Lambe 978-1-78952-004-0
David Cronenberg – Patrick Chapman 978-1-78952-071-2
Doctor Who: The David Tennant Years – Jamie Hailstone 978-1-78952-066-8
James Bond – Andrew Wild 978-1-78952-010-1
Monty Python – Steve Pilkington 978-1-78952-047-7
Seinfeld Seasons 1 to 5 – Stephen Lambe 978-1-78952-012-5

Other Books
1967: A Year In Psychedelic Rock 978-1-78952-155-9
1970: A Year In Rock – John Van der Kiste 978-1-78952-147-4
1973: The Golden Year of Progressive Rock 978-1-78952-165-8
Babysitting A Band On The Rocks – G.D. Praetorius 978-1-78952-106-1
Eric Clapton Sessions – Andrew Wild 978-1-78952-177-1
Derek Taylor: For Your Radioactive Children –
Andrew Darlington 978-1-78952-038-5
The Golden Road: The Recording History of The Grateful Dead – John Kilbride 978-1-78952-156-6
Iggy and The Stooges On Stage 1967-1974 – Per Nilsen 978-1-78952-101-6
Jon Anderson and the Warriors – the road to Yes –
David Watkinson 978-1-78952-059-0
Magic: The David Paton Story – David Paton 978-1-78952-266-2
Misty: The Music of Johnny Mathis – Jakob Baekgaard 978-1-78952-247-1
Nu Metal: A Definitive Guide – Matt Karpe 978-1-78952-063-7
Tommy Bolin: In and Out of Deep Purple – Laura Shenton 978-1-78952-070-5
Maximum Darkness – Deke Leonard 978-1-78952-048-4
The Twang Dynasty – Deke Leonard 978-1-78952-049-1

and many more to come!

Would you like to write for Sonicbond Publishing?

At Sonicbond Publishing we are always on the look-out for authors, particularly for our two main series:

On Track. Mixing fact with in depth analysis, the On Track series examines the work of a particular musical artist or group. All genres are considered from easy listening and jazz to 60s soul to 90s pop, via rock and metal.

On Screen. This series looks at the world of film and television. Subjects considered include directors, actors and writers, as well as entire television and film series. As with the On Track series, we balance fact with analysis.

While professional writing experience would, of course, be an advantage the most important qualification is to have real enthusiasm and knowledge of your subject. First-time authors are welcomed, but the ability to write well in English is essential.

Sonicbond Publishing has distribution throughout Europe and North America, and all books are also published in E-book form. Authors will be paid a royalty based on sales of their book.

Further details are available from www.sonicbondpublishing.co.uk. To contact us, complete the contact form there or email info@sonicbondpublishing.co.uk